Frederick Thomas Kruckenberg

A thought and a prayer for every day in the year

Frederick Thomas Kruckenberg

A thought and a prayer for every day in the year

ISBN/EAN: 9783741179440

Manufactured in Europe, USA, Canada, Australia, Japa

Cover: Foto ©Andreas Hilbeck / pixelio.de

Manufactured and distributed by brebook publishing software (www.brebook.com)

Frederick Thomas Kruckenberg

A thought and a prayer for every day in the year

A THOUGHT AND A PRAYER

FOR

EVERY DAY IN THE YEAR.

A Thought and a Prayer

FOR

Every Day in the Year.

BY

F. T. KRUCKENBERG, A.K.C.,

VICAR OF GREWELTHORPE.

WITH PREFACE BY THE VERY REV.

E. H. PLUMPTRE, D.D.,

DEAN OF WELLS.

London:
SKEFFINGTON & SON, 103, PICCADILLY.
1885.

Preface.

EXPERIENCE seems to show that it is a help to many minds to have subjects for daily meditation and prayer suggested to them from without. Texts from Scripture, as in the "Daily Steps towards Heaven," or "The Words of the Lord Jesus," and reflections rising out of them—maxims and thoughts from the great Masters of the Devout Life, à Kempis, Augustine, Francis de Sales, Bishop Ken, Bishop Wilson—these, in manifold variety of combination, have ministered to the wants of thousands.

The little work which is now presented to the Reader is framed on a different model. I have not tested it by the continued use which is the only adequate criterion in such matters ; what I have read of it, however, seems enough to justify me in commending it, without entering into any comparison of its merits with those of other Manuals of a like kind, as fitted to build up the character of those who use it, in the self-knowledge, the earnestness, the aspirations after a higher life, of which it is manifestly the outcome.

E. H. PLUMPTRE.

Deanery, Wells, Somerset,
  Oct. 29th, 1885.

A THOUGHT AND A PRAYER

FOR

EVERY DAY IN THE YEAR.

January 1st. (Circumcision.)

During the year, let us do all that we can to go forward in personal religion, let us be given to more sober thought —more fervent prayer—more frequent Communions—more godly work, valuing our Christian calling, our Bible—our Church. Let us see whether we cannot make some real progress—there must be motion—oh, that it may not be backwards, but forwards!—*Lord, make me to grow in grace, give me steadiness of purpose, and grant that I may strive earnestly.*

January 2nd.

All things human change, let us go to the home of our infancy and see the place that knew us as children—changes everywhere—sorrow almost fills the heart, we think we could scarcely be happy there again. Above there is One, our Heavenly Father, Who has watched all these changes, Who Himself has not changed, He calls us onward to an eternal Home.—*O everliving God, surely fix my heart where true joys are to be found.*

January 3rd.

God's eternity is a happy subject for thought, for it speaks of a blessed eternity for those who are His. Surely we do not look upon ourselves as mere creatures of time. Do we not feel something of immortality, as we lay hold upon Him Who is our eternal portion? Do we not feel, that with God as our God, there can be no interruption to our being?—*Hold me, O God, in Thine everlasting arms.*

A

January 4th.

As fellow-creatures, fellow-Christians, fellow-travellers, there ought to be fellow-feeling amongst us. Do we differ so much in character and circumstances, that such seems out of the question? Surely not. Christianity holds forth to us the kindliness of Christ for our imitation—let us gaze on Christ, as set before us in the Gospels, and let some of His tender-heartedness be reflected from ourselves.—*Give me, Lord Jesus, a practical and a growing sympathy.*

January 5th.

We are not going to be saved by our feelings. God sometimes sees fit to withhold from us the comforts of religion—it is for us to attend to its duties and to make our endeavours to please our Heavenly Father very real. Let us bravely take God at His word—never let us be tempted to think wrongly of Him—He is the faithful One Who has promised.—*O Lord, in Thee have I trusted, oh, save me!*

January 6th. (Epiphany.)

At the Epiphany we think of the glory of the Lord Jesus, His divine nature, the Godhead of our incarnate King. Lest we should be lost in contemplation of the divine brightness, our Church is continuously reminding us, during this Season, of simple duties, setting before us some most practical precepts (in the Epistles for the Sundays after the Epiphany) by which to rule our daily conduct.—*Jesus, my King, grant that I may serve Thee in everyday life.*

January 7th.

How many false notions there are of rest. Work here on earth, for the most part, leads to weariness, but hereafter we may work and yet never tire—we may rest and yet never be idle. We must seek to enter into that rest which is to be found in Christ. True rest does not depend so much upon outward circumstances—it is to have a quiet mind—the mind of Christ.—*Fit me, good Lord, to do Christian work, and to enjoy Christian rest.*

January 8th.

Before we can be really happy, we want to know true life—we want to know what it is truly to live. What is to be compared to true life—the life of the soul—the life which is divine! How happy to know a life above the world, conscious of the powers of the world to come—to be partakers of the spiritual life!—*O Christ, live in me as my life.*

January 9th.

We should strive to make our worship of God the best that we can offer—we should be careful that it should not be lacking in any of its component parts. There must be thanksgiving and praise as well as prayer and petition. We ought to think of this in our private devotions—as for our public worship we have a form of words, ready for our use, which has stood the test of ages.—*Lord, open Thou our lips.*

January 10th.

Union with Christ is the great blessing which the Sacraments of the Gospel offer—this is something more than the promise of Christ's presence—goes far beyond it. Those who have received the one Sacrament—have put on Christ in Baptism—ought regularly to come to the other—to the Sacrament of the Lord's Supper, to feed upon Christ Who not only died for us, but lives to be our life.—*Lord Jesus, live in me, and claim me for Thine own.*

January 11th.

Many there are who would not like to be thought ignorant of other subjects, who are yet not ashamed to be found ignorant of what the Bible teaches. We ought to put the study of Holy Scripture before every other study, because of its importance. Let us pray God to incline us to be more desirous of knowing the truth.—*Instruct me, O God, and grant that I may walk in Thy ways with a perfect heart.*

January 12th.

If we look upon Jesus as our Teacher, shall we not value His teaching and try to carry it out? Shall we not find ourselves striving to live as He did? Shall not our homes be the happier if Christ's teaching be attended to, mutual duties being more thoroughly fulfilled? Whatever our position in the world or in the family may be, we may learn from the great Master.—*Teach me, Lord Jesus, the lesson that I need most.*

January 13th

Our Lord Jesus Christ said to His disciples not merely "Love one another," but added "as I have loved you." The old law of love which dated from the beginning was thus made a new commandment—renewed in Him. We see, then, looking to Jesus, what our love should be like. To see love in the life is far better than having only a description of it.—*Teach me, Lord Jesus, Thy self-sacrificing love.*

January 14th.

On earth there are to be found those who know Christ, and those who know Him not—those who follow Christ, and those who follow Him not. There are some who profess to know Christ without following Him, but their knowledge is vain. It is no good merely to think and mean well—we must be eager to act—active in following.—*Grant, Lord Jesus, that, by following Thee, I may grow in the knowledge of Thee, to my great comfort and happiness.*

January 15th.

Our connection with others at home and abroad—our life, in the family and in the world, should furnish us with matter for prayer. How many things may give occasion to the Christian to pray! Do we not love our fellows? Are we not interested in what goes on around us? Shall we not pray? Can we be happy, and live as brethren, without frequent intercourse with the Father of us all?—*Make me to delight, O God, in prayer.*

January 16th.

The surface of the sea undergoes much change from day to day, but there is stillness in the depths; even so will it be with the Christian. It will never do for us to pass through life without calm, steady thought. Let our meditations be earnest and fervent—let them be frequent, though they be but short. It becomes us all to think seriously of death and judgment, heaven and hell.—*O my God, may I think on these things to my profit.*

January 17th.

How timid we are of confessing Christ before men as we ought, shewing ourselves to be on His side! We are all, verily, guilty of this in a greater or less degree. Let us strive to have such a correct knowledge of that which is right and good and true that, by the help of God's grace, we may be proof against even seeming, on any occasion, to side with the false and the evil.—*Lord, strengthen me to stand.*

January 18th.

In life we, for the most part, find that we have just enough encouragement to carry us forward—there seems continually something to allure us on and to give us zest. At length experience teaches the lesson which it seems cannot be learnt in any other way, it is this—I am a stranger upon earth—my inheritance is in Heaven. God has been educating us.—*Teach me, Lord God, to pray " Thy Kingdom come."*

January 19th.

We must beware of the force of habit and custom—we may soon get into bad habits—we may soon be led away by foolish customs. We must know, too, that with God there is no sheltering ourselves under the plea that all is according to the fashions of the day. It is not enough to say that we merely do as others do.—*Teach me, my divine Master, to know and do the right.*

January 20th.

It is not intended that we should be all alike—as a fact there is much variety amongst us. Though we may have much in common, we have different strong points and different weaknesses. We must each seek special grace to conquer our special faults, to work out that life which God has given us, and which, rightly led, will, in its own way, redound to His glory.—*Grant, Lord, that I may bear much fruit.*

January 21st.

How often do we hear people say, "there is no harm in it," yet there may be harm in it! We ought to try to be very real Christians, and very decidedly on the side of what is true and right. Have we a good hope for the future? Does our practice at all interfere with, or bedim the brightness of our hope?—*God, grant that I may so love Thee, that I may be intent on obeying Thee.*

January 22nd.

The nearer we live to this world, the more distant will the next seem to us—the more real we esteem this, the more shadowy will the future world appear—the more worldly we become, the less shall we be like Christ—making this present world our home, we shall be in danger of forgetting our Father's home above.—*Help me, Lord, to live as a traveller and foreigner here, and so pass on.*

January 23rd.

Be content. You may look around you and see dishonesty thrive, you may see iniquity succeed, you may see the wicked prosper—but what is that to thee? "Take that thine is, and go thy way." Wait a little while, be patient, be bravely patient. Look above and beyond the present state of things.—*Jesus, Master, Lord and Saviour, bid me be of good cheer.*

January 24th.

Doctrinal facts form the basis of, and are the motive and incentive to, all godly living. To separate doctrine from practice is to sever that which God has joined together. The practice of religion will always thrive in proportion as its doctrines are understood and firmly received and believed, and practice will degenerate and decay in proportion as the doctrines are misunderstood and neglected.—*Lord, may I see the force of the therefores, wherefores, thens and ifs of S. Paul's Epistles.*

January 25th. (Conversion of S. Paul.)

God reigns over the hearts of men, and His grace is daily accomplishing wonders—hearts are being changed and sanctified. We must remember that he, who attributed his conversion to the grace of God, has told us that he was not disobedient to the vision which he saw, but surrendered himself to his Lord. He did not resist, or quench, or grieve the Holy Spirit.—*Visit me with Thy salvation, and take not Thy Holy Spirit from me.*

January 26th.

As there is unity in the body of the individual, so ought there to be unity among Christians. We are members of Christ, limbs of His body. As the limbs of the natural body work in harmony, because they are all in subjection and obedience to one will, so must Christians work in harmony, realizing the unity of the Spirit, having for the most part the same objects in view, the same interests at heart, being of one mind.—*Lord Jesus, may we be one !*

January 27th.

Christianity is eminently practical. As Christians, we should think much of action—action based on Christian principles, the fruit of Christianity. A theoretical and a practical knowledge are two very different things. We should learn to walk in a Christian manner amongst men, and put all that we have learnt into practice.—*O God, teach me to be a practical Christian.*

January 28th.

Examine yourself concerning your hope. Is yours a true or a false hope? When alone, apart from others, unoccupied, look into your heart and see if you have a good hope. In the time of adversity—when any misfortune has befallen you—any reverse come across your path, or in the time of sickness, see to it whether you have a good hope.—*Lord, I would neither despair of, nor presume in Thy mercy, give me a lively hope in Thee.*

January 29th.

The Lord Jesus has assured us that He will be one with His people. The drawing near to Him by faith, in the ways in which He has promised to be found, will lead to our knowing more of Him, and the more we know of Him, the more shall we imitate Him, and the more we imitate Him, the more fit shall we become for His more immediate presence.—*O Lord, ripen me for Heaven.*

January 30th.

Beware of self-love! Beware of anger! Beware of pride! Each of these is of a nature such as to prevent our seeing the conduct of others aright—a magnifying glass, a curved mirror, a false medium cannot be worse or more misleading. We must pray for the single eye, the calm judgment, the spirit which should characterize the Christian.—*Lord, make me just and honest and righteous in my dealings with others.*

January 31st.

Am I learning to realize by faith the world unseen? Am I viewing this world as I ought—looking at it from a Christian stand-point? Have I learnt to take a right estimate of humanity? Am I growing into a more perfect man? Am I thinking more often and more carefully about my duty? Am I loving God more and more, knowing Him better, and finding greater pleasure in His service?—*Teach me, O God, to examine myself.*

February 1st.

Man's work and activity will be of no avail without God's blessing. We sometimes think too highly of our own efforts. Yet no system devised by man, however great may be the pains taken with it in drawing it up and carrying it out, unless blessed by God, can issue in any good results. God must have His place in all undertakings, we want His sanction and His smile.—*Direct me, Lord, and help me in all good works.*

February 2nd. (Purification of the Virgin Mary.)

The little child teaches us, let us also help to teach the little child. We ourselves are taught by what we may call the natural graces of childhood. The child wants from us (besides the divine blessing) guidance, correction, assistance, instruction—these we must be prepared to give out of love to Him Who, for our sakes, became the Babe of Bethlehem to make us new creatures and children of God.—*Grant me, Lord God, the daily renewing of Thy Holy Spirit.*

February 3rd.

Oh, might it be ours to live in the realized presence of God! How happy to be continually looking up to Him, and to desire His eye to be upon us! There are sacred feelings in the human heart which can be understood by none so well as by God—which He understands, and which He can explain to us. There are wants, too, which none other can supply in such divine fulness.—*Dwell in me, O God.*

February 4th.

Do we delight in our Sundays—are they helping us to sanctify the whole week—are they preparing us for, and pointing us to, the time when types and shadows shall cease ? Are our affections becoming sanctified—our wills more in conformity with God's will ? Does Heaven appear more near ?—our hearts must be in Heaven before we can hope to go there. How can we answer these questions ?—*Fit me, O God, for eternal Sabbath-keeping.*

February 5th.

We need from others a great deal of love and sympathy —at least, it is so with most of us (with some it may be otherwise, some may be able to live very much alone), and what we ourselves prize, we should be ready to offer to others. God has constituted us members of families, so that our affections may be gradually expanded, and that there may be much precious giving and receiving of the heart's best gifts.—*Lord, I have received, so incline me to give.*

February 6th.

We know not what may befall us as we go forward in religion—how many surprises may overtake us—with how many difficulties we may meet, but we know that it is our duty to proceed. We shall never make progress in the Christian life unless we learn to act in faith, doing present duty, trusting for the future—making good resolutions, and seeking by God's help to carry them out.—*Draw me, Lord, and I will come after Thee.*

February 7th.

Let us all see what we can do for God, for is there not something special in everyone's stewardship—something which God would have done by each of us which cannot be done so well by another? Without being in the least degree proud or high-minded, but only filled with a keen sense of individual responsibility, earnestly desirous of doing my part, may I not deem this to be the case?—*Lord, set me my work.*

February 8th.

We should think that child a very selfish and disagreeable one who only spoke when wanting something, and yet this is the way in which many treat God—this is the very inadequate view which many often take of prayer. The aim of the true Christian is assuredly to enjoy intercourse and communion with God, as his Father in Heaven.—*Make me happy, Lord, in Thy presence, speaking from my heart to Thee.*

February 9th.

How much we gain by placing ourselves on our knees before God—speaking to our good Father—looking away from earth to Heaven. On the other hand, how much we lose by scantiness of prayer, bringing about as it does the dying within us of all real desire after God and communion with Him. We gain and lose much by cultivating or not cultivating habits of devotion.—*Train me, O God, to keep my face Heavenward.*

February 10th.

We find it difficult to carry religion into everyday life—to serve God in little things. The very absence in them of the look of importance throws us off our guard—we attempt them in our own strength, and fail. In greater and less common matters, seemingly of more importance, we seek divine help. Very subtle is the temptation to forget our need of God's aid in little things.—*Grant, Lord, that I may seek to please Thee in everything.*

February 11th.

The Christian, having learnt the law of love, seeks to hide the faults of his neighbours instead of blazing them abroad, as is the custom with so many. The humble follower of Jesus ever tries to make allowance for, and to cover the multitude of sins. It is no sign of personal holiness to talk about the misdoings of others. We must cultivate the grace of Christian love.—*Keep me, O God, from being a talebearer.*

February 12th.

How often do we seek to be alone—if only for a brief space—with an all-sympathising God! "Enter into thy closet," saith our Divine Master. There is something in the constitution of our nature which seems to render it necessary that we should sometimes get away from others to be quiet, full of thought and prayer.—*In this, as in other things, incline me, Lord Jesus, to follow Thy example.*

February 13th.

How many of us make our arrangements in a sinfully selfish manner. The calls of religion can be attended to, when they do not interfere with what we often love more than anything else—self-gratification. How good will it be when we see real self-interest and duty to be one, and when we learn to delight in God's service, be it the service of our daily life, or the service of the sanctuary!—*Lead me, O my God, to better things.*

February 14th.

God does not ask of us anything that is impossible—even when we do not understand all that is implied in the command, we must try to obey, looking for divine help which will surely be given, if sought. We shall be happier in striving simply to obey, than in achieving all manner of worldly success, for we shall feel that in obeying, we are preparing ourselves for the great Hereafter.—*Father, make me an obedient child.*

February 15th.

Do we ever find ourselves sinning against the spirit of a divine command, when conscience will not allow us to break it literally? Do we ever keep looking at things from different points of view, trying to persuade ourselves that wrong is not far from right—such conduct shows want of singleness of heart—want of love to God. We may successfully deceive ourselves, but we cannot deceive God.—*Make me honest with myself, O God, and true to Thee.*

February 16th.

Do not let any be discouraged by the thought that they can do but little good in the world, and that but little will come of their efforts. The result of our work will ever appear insignificant—the good which we may be able to effect in life will ever seem trifling, but that is no reason why we should withhold our hand—it behoves us to do what we can.—*Grant me diligence in every good work, O God.*

February 17th.

How welcome is the bidding to lift up the heart! How good is it to lift up our hearts to the Lord—to seek from above strength to resist temptation, and to do our work—to cast cares and anxieties on one side—to leave off fretting—to rise above the sorrows and annoyances of earth—to become more spiritually minded, and to hold communion with God!—*Draw my heart Heavenward, O Lord, of Thy great goodness.*

February 18th.

If we seek faithfully, devoutly and diligently, we shall not fail by God's grace to attain to His promises, for He is faithful that has promised. We must not wander about here and there, at the mercy of circumstances, without fixedness of purpose—without definiteness of aim—without strength of resolution. We must take each event and duty as it comes, and bend all to our service, making everything a means of grace.—*Lord, help me to press toward the mark.*

February 19th.

By following the example of Christ, we grow more heavenly-minded, and testify to others of that Heaven which we hope to reach. If we learn from the Lord Jesus, and shew what we have learnt by the manner of our lives, how good will it be! We have all some truth to teach—we must try to teach something of Christ in our lives, and to set an example which shall never die.—*Master, use me for Thy glory.*

February 20th.

God can work in any way He pleases, but ordinarily He bestows His gifts through the means of grace; so that if we do not use the means, we have no right to suppose that He will give us His grace. Though Christ may communicate Himself to the individual soul by *other* means, the *appointed* means cannot be lightly esteemed by those who would seek their soul's welfare.—*Grant, O Saviour of men, that I may be led to use all the helps Thou hast given to Thy Church.*

February 29th.

As we are differently constituted and have different capabilities, so we may be suited for different work. Exercising our own particular gifts, we may each do something for the common profit, glad to do what we can. In the building up of the Christian Church, it matters little on what part of the building we are engaged, so long as we build rightly and faithfully on the true foundation.—*What can I do, good Lord, for Thee?*

March 1st.

Great results may spring from seemingly very little things—little acts of thoughtlessness, carelessness, and disobedience. One single act—one little act is often mighty in its influence over the whole life. What importance does this thought give to our actions! What a solemn thing does life seem! Acts once done are sometimes never remedied—we may never be able to undo what we have foolishly done.—*Lord, have mercy upon me, and save me from myself.*

March 2nd.

We never know when the attack of the Evil One may be made, so we must seek always to be prepared for it. We never know what trials and temptations may be coming upon us, so we must be watchful, lest, coming suddenly upon us, they surprise us. We must take care not to be overtaken in a fault—not to let Satan have an advantage over us.—*Make me, good Lord, to watch and pray lest I fall.*

March 3rd.

The formation of character is gradual—it is forming every day, though it is only perhaps now and then that something happens to reveal it. How watchful and careful should we ever be! The little words and little acts of each hour are most important, they give tone to the life. We must take heed that worldliness creep not upon us unawares.—*Enable me to be, O God, what Thou wouldest have me to be.*

February 25th.

There are different stages of Christian growth. We must not rest satisfied in the mere beginnings, but strive to improve, looking forward to the time when hope shall be changed into certainty, and faith into sight—when grace shall give place to glory—things temporal to things eternal—when the Christian shall be no longer wearied with manifold temptations, but at rest in Christ —*Holy Father, lead Thou me on.*

February 26th.

Professedly, we have all renounced the world, the flesh, and the devil. Have we actually done so? There is not that difference between the life of the Churchman and the life of the worldling that there ought to be. What is the remedy? See what it was that animated those of old time. It was faith—conviction of the truth. When we have faith like theirs, then, too, may our lives be like theirs.— *Lord, I would walk by faith, help me.*

February 27th.

We must thank and praise God for what Christ has done for us, and we must seek strength that we may do something for God in the world. In the case of each one of us there is a work to be done, let us set Christ, the beloved Son, before us as our example, and seek the Holy Spirit's help that we may follow Him, the Sacrifice for our sins.—*Lord Jesus, make me a Christian indeed.*

February 28th.

We may know that we have the hearty good wishes of all around us, and yet we may feel that something is wanting. Some of the yearnings of man, God alone can fully supply. Unless we are at peace with God, we shall feel a void within, which nothing earthly is able to satisfy.—*O God, fill this heart of mine with Thy love.*

March 8th.

Never let us neglect regular self-examination. We shall have only a faint idea of our extreme sinfulness, unless we look seriously within, and are taught by the Holy Spirit of God to know ourselves. How good will it be, if, convinced of sin, we throw ourselves more entirely on the Saviour, and seek more earnestly that grace without which there is no true life!—*With self-knowledge, O God, give me also the knowledge of my Saviour.*

March 9th.

In the hour of temptation, let us think of Christ Jesus, our Saviour and our King, so may we be saved at the critical moment—held back from sin. Let us seek strength not to lose courage, but to persevere, trying in the daily walk of life to keep in the sunshine of the Divine Presence.—*Save me and help me, good Lord.*

March 10th.

It is the grace of God alone which can enable us to perceive our sin. Those who live without God in the world do not feel their guilt. It requires the Holy Spirit of God, speaking to the conscience, to awaken the knowledge of sin within—to present it before us in all its wretchedness and hatefulness. The presence or absence of a sense of sinfulness, we may take as a test of our spiritual condition.—*Deliver me, good Lord, from blindness of heart.*

March 11th.

Perseveringly try to obey ; and you will, God helping you, succeed at last. You may have to struggle, and may have many a stumble in the way, but, repenting and believing, you must not lose courage. Do your best to overcome the difficulties which lie in your path, and the more consistently you act, the brighter will be your life.—*Make me, O Father, weak as I am, a loving, trusting, and obedient child.*

March 12th.

What a reproof do the busy ones of earth, who find much time for prayer and holy intercourse with God, give to those who are always saying " we have no time "— how much better do these do their work—how many more are the victories which they gain—how much more firmly do they stand in the evil day, thus shewing the secret of their strength!—*Make me, good Lord, a witness in the world for Thee.*

March 13th.

God does not mean this world to be gloomy and sad at every turn. Though ever bearing the future in mind, the Christian is open to the enjoyment of the present. Happy is the man who, divinely taught, can make a prudent use of all things, and, by the help of grace, overcome the difficulties which oppose themselves, animated with a buoyant hope!—*Make me to be mindful, Lord, both of Thy example, and Thy merits.*

March 14th.

It may be we shall never realize here, how greatly we have been dependent upon outward forms for the sustenance of our religious life. It is vain and presumptuous for any of us to think ourselves so spiritual and so independent of externals, as to be able to live as we ought without the helps which the visible Church of Christ offers to us.— *Make me, O God, truly humble in myself, and truly strong in Thee.*

March 15th.

If you have any regard to your own spiritual life, and the spiritual life of others, take heed to your tongue— speech is the gift of God. Like other things which a good Creator has given us, it may be abused, instead of being used to the glory of the Giver. Speak as in the presence of God Who loves truth, purity, and kindness.—*Set a watch, O Lord, before my mouth, and keep the door of my lips.*

March 16th.

There is nothing that ought to give greater satisfaction and gladness to the Christian than the seeing evil subdued, and goodness gaining ground. Each little triumph of the Kingdom of Light over the Kingdom of Darkness should give us real pleasure, and be to us a pledge of the final overthrow of the Devil's Kingdom, and the perfecting of the Kingdom of Christ.—*Subdue, good Lord, the evil within me—overcome in me the sins which beset me.*

March 17th.

There has ever been found great peril in idleness. The Devil calls men into his service when he sees them idle. He has then his opportunity. It is well for us to have plenty to do. Blessed shall we be, in the midst of all our employments, if we do all under the shadow of the Cross—in the name of the Lord Jesus—to the glory of God !—*Save me, O Lord, from being slothful in business.*

March 18th.

Holy exercises are not to draw us away from the duties of life's calling—not to lead us to perform those duties less well. Regular attendance at Church and at the Holy Table—frequent reading of God's Word—solemn private prayer—self-examination and meditation—all these are means of grace which, faithfully used, will enable us to do better work in the world. It is certain that the life of good deeds can only be sustained by communion with God.—*O God, give me Christian energy.*

March 19th.

In the good news of the Gospel, there is to be found no pretext for idleness or inactivity—no encouragement to sin. The goodness of God is to lead us to repentance and godly living. Motives for holiness are supplied to us in Christ, and spiritual strength will be ministered to us, if we seek it, to live as children of our good Father in Heaven. —*May Thy love, O Christ, constrain us, and Thy grace, O Holy Spirit, help us.*

March 20th.

Our danger often lies in little things, we may grow less religious by degrees, and become worldly almost without knowing it—by little and little. Let us look on the other side of the picture—as it is the little things which endanger man's salvation, so is it the little things which help to make the saint. By paying attention to little things, we may grow in holiness.—*Teach me, O Lord, to be very watchful.*

March 21st.

We rely too much upon our own exertions—we do not think enough of God. Thus we do dishonour to the great Enabler, and work becomes restlessness. We can understand the busy bustle of the world, but we do not enter fully into the meaning of the quiet time of devotion, which fits us for active service. We are doing real good to ourselves and to others, when praying to God.—*Work in me, good Lord.*

March 22nd.

We know that we have difficulties in life to contend with—do not let us complain. We sometimes think, perhaps, that it would have been best that men should have been made at once what they were ultimately intended to be, but it is not for us to judge—God is wise. Our fitness for another life is to be attained by fighting against the things which oppose us—offering resistance to evil.—*Good Lord, strengthen me, and preserve me.*

March 23rd.

May we not blot out our past sins by serving God for the future? No. We must look to the finished work of Christ for that—there is no such thing as creature merit; but what will follow?—hearty belief in the great Atonement will urge us on to strive to please God. Those who trust in Christ love to follow Him in the path of holy obedience.—*Grant, O Father, that faith in my Saviour may lead to holiness and purity in my life.*

March 24th.

Set Christ crucified daily before your eyes—be not shaken in the great doctrine of the Atonement. Pray to know the burden of sin, and the blessedness of relief—to feel your need of the Saviour, and to rejoice in finding Him. Our natural pride rebels against the truth, but try to be humble Christians, to be childlike, to receive the Scriptural account of man's redemption.—*God forbid that I should glory, save in the Cross of our Lord Jesus Christ!*

March 25th. (Annunciation of the Virgin Mary.)

Gabriel standing in the presence of God—doing Him homage—beholding His face. What a picture! He is ready, as a servant, to do God's will—to fulfil any errand that might be entrusted to him. How happy must he have felt, when sent to the Virgin at Nazareth to announce the incarnation of Him Who was to partake of the human, that we might partake of the divine nature.—*O Father, make me a bearer of some message for Thee, concerning Jesus.*

March 26th.

Faith in God is the foundation of all true life, and lies at the root of all good deeds. Faith will meet with its trials—hence perseverance is required. Any lack of perseverance shews a want of faith in God, and may lead to irretrievable loss. Let us endeavour to be faithful to our Christian calling.—*Suffer us not, good Lord, in the time of temptation to fall away.*

March 27th.

We have been taught to thank God for "the means of grace." Do we use them aright—each one singly—each in its place—neglecting none—using all as one divinely-appointed whole? Each has its office towards the furtherance of the Christian life, and there is a connection between them all. How much depends upon our conduct in this matter!—*O God, bid me humbly come to Thee through Jesus Christ.*

March 28th.

We must seek to glorify God both with our lips and in our lives. In this busy age when all is activity, and business occupies so much time, we are, many of us, in danger of forgetting the service of prayer, thanksgiving and praise, and then our activity ceases to be Christian work. On the other hand, we must not forget that we owe God active service—devotion of the life as well as the service of the Sanctuary.—*O God, enable me to worship and to work.*

March 29th.

If we look to Jesus as our King, how ready shall we be to use every opportunity of worshipping Him—of paying Him due homage! How desirous—how anxious shall we be always to live as His faithful subjects—obeying His laws—shewing loving submission to His will; and as we live and labour on, as those seeking to be approved, how hopefully shall we pray " Thy Kingdom come " !—*Bless me in present, and fit me, Lord, for future service.*

March 30th.

The Christian looks not for merit in himself, but in Christ—his work is a work of love, not a work for wages. We must not look upon our works (or even our faith or our repentance) as having any merit. We are suppliants before God—the humbler we are the better, as we look to Jesus, our dear Lord, and consider what He has done for us.— *God, be merciful to me a sinner.*

March 31st.

The Sacrament of the Lord's Supper was called by the early Christians " the perfecting Service," implying that it was the highest means of grace, to be used by those who were striving to attain to full growth. All true life is progressive. The Christian is one who is continually looking forward—pressing toward the mark—taking no low aim— following Christ.—*Lord Jesus, bid me follow Thee—speak the word of power to me.*

April 1st.

What a happiness it is to have a sense of freedom, to feel as if we were getting free from sin and from fear—to feel free to work and free to look to Heaven for knowledge and for strength—to feel free-men—Christians ; to feel that we have chosen God's service which is perfect freedom—Christian liberty—the glorious liberty of the children of God !—*Lord Jesus, make me free indeed.*

April 2nd.

Is there not joy in striving to serve God ? Though we may meet with but poor success, yet, when we are sincerely doing our best to break off any evil practice, the very consciousness that we are engaged in the battle against sin, which God hates, gives us pleasure. We must never let Satan tempt us to despair—in the strength of God we must go on to better things.—*Bless me, O my Father, in all my efforts after good.*

April 3rd.

Our spiritual crucifixion, burial, and resurrection with Christ are no acts done once for all, but progressive work. Only by continual striving can we live up to our Christian privileges, and do our Christian duties aright. Day by day we must die to sin, become more truly separated from the sinful, and rise to newness of life here, having a good hope of the Hereafter.—*Help me, O God, passing through life's varied experiences, to attain to true life.*

April 4th.

Do we need any incentive to work ?—we have it in this ; we are not our own, but creatures of the great Creator, bought with the price of the spotless Lamb of God—this is the true incentive to work. Let us do all, as a work of duty and a work of love, in the strength of God's Holy Spirit. We humbly give God of His own.—*Quicken me, O Lord, according as Thou art wont.*

April 5th.

What is the character of Christ's Kingdom? It is not like the Kingdoms of this world to be maintained by the sword. There have been those who have sought to propagate religion by force, but it is not so in the Kingdom of Christ. Compulsion with the Christian becomes persuasion—the soldier of Christ relies not on physical, but on moral and spiritual power.—*Set Thy mark upon me, O God, that I may ever be known as Thine.*

April 6th.

When one really embraces Christianity, there must needs be a contrast between oneself and the mere lukewarm professor. The hearty reception of Christianity is mighty in its results, new friends—new foes—new loves—new hates appear upon the scene, one's judgment concerning things is changed—a new world is opened up to one—enlarged privileges and new duties make themselves known—the battle of life is realized—there is a longing for victory.—*O God, speak to my heart, and claim it for Thine own.*

April 7th.

Is there no real work for God to do in life? Is there no call for exertion on our part? Yes, surely. Dare we be spiritually idle, when life is so short—when Christian duties are so many—when the Devil is so active—when the Church needs our energy—when our own life is such as it is, and when others have need of encouragement! It will never do to dream.—*Bid me, Lord, be up and doing.*

April 8th.

Who is there who has not had dark hours—who has not been puzzled at the mystery of creature-existence? Who is there who has not, amid the anxieties and cares of life—wishes disappointed—love ill-requited—affections doubted—words and acts misunderstood, had some misgivings concerning the world to come, of which the Bible speaks to us?—*Never let faith and hope be stifled in me, good Lord, nor let me lose touch of the world unseen.*

April 9th.

There is much wrong-doing in the world which God seems to pass over—which God seems, as it were, to wink at—but this is only for a time. Forbearance has, Scripture teaches us, a limit; there is a point at which God's long-suffering ends, and judgment begins—a time after which the Holy Spirit ceases to strive, having been resisted so often, and so long.—*Make me quickly to obey, good Spirit, Thy godly motions.*

April 10th.

True humility will not lead to idleness—we make a great mistake when we put forward humility as an excuse for sloth. Genuine humility is learnt upon the knees, and prompts us to work diligently and trustfully, aiming at personal holiness, and seeking to do good—active in the present—hopeful for the future—thinking of God's glory rather than of self.—*Make me, Lord, humble and useful.*

April 11th.

God deals with us in different ways. Sometimes He allows us to wander, and calls us back from a far country to our home—sometimes He leads us up a very gradual ascent closer and closer to Himself. So, too, has He different ways of bringing His influence to bear upon us—sometimes by revealing the greatness of His love—sometimes by shewing us the emptiness and vanity of the world.—*Nearer my God to Thee, nearer to Thee!*

April 12th.

We need not only *stirring up*—the Christian life wants *building up*. Nothing short of godly principle—a surrendering of ourselves to God in heart and life will suffice. Excitement—good feelings—lively impressions will not do—religion does not consist in these; we want something stronger and more lasting to stand the scrutiny of the reckoning at the Great Day.—*Make me, O Lord, a more perfect Christian.*

April 13th.

Though it is well to realize our individuality before God, that truth of our individuality would at times be almost intolerable, were it not for the counterbalancing truth that we are members one of another. How often do we want the help and encouragement of others—or, at least, to feel them near, and to know that in some sort they sympathize with us!—*Enable me, O Lord, to give to others the sympathy which I crave.*

April 14th.

If we look to Jesus as our Saviour, our life here will be influenced for good, and this in proportion as He is acknowledged by us. Clothed with humility, we shall learn to shew forth a self-sacrificing love. Trustfully reposing on the Saviour's merits, we shall go forth daily to work in His strength. Though sins may weigh heavily upon us, knowing Him as the Sin-bearer, we shall never lose hope.—*Blessed Jesus, help me to spell out the meaning of Thy Name.*

April 15th.

We cannot do without trials—they have formed a part of God's discipline from the first. The time will come when sickness, pain, affliction and the like, brought into the world by sin. having served God's purpose, shall be done away; and they who have, with patience, humbled themselves, shall be comforted and exalted. Shall our trials tend to make us more like Christ?—*Lord Jesus, Prince of Sufferers, make me like Thyself.*

April 16th.

If we are seeking to be divinely blest, we must put ourselves, as it were, into the proper attitude for receiving the divine blessing—Zaccheus climbed up into the sycamore, because he knew our Lord was to pass that way. We know the different ways in which we may look for our God, and expect to meet Him.—*Urge me, good Lord, to make faithful trial of all the means of grace.*

April 17th.

We may do somewhat of our duty at all times, but there are times when we may do more direct work for Christ. Each one of us may do some special work. Ask God in prayer what it shall be, and obey His call which may come in the way of suggestion, perhaps, or almost unconscious desire; then give yourself to the work.—*Father, teach me what to do for Thee.*

April 18th.

In the present day there are many who seem to think that no matter what we believe, if we only act up to it, all will be well—in other words, that any religion, conscientiously carried out, will be acceptable in God's sight. This is not the teaching of Holy Scripture which sets before us *Jesus* as the Name of our Salvation.—*Help me, gracious God, to keep steadfast in the Faith.*

April 19th.

The conviction of sin, like the knowledge of one's ignorance, is the first step towards improvement; yet, if we had this without the consolation of God's Holy Spirit, we should be overwhelmed, it may be, with overmuch sorrow—we should lack that cheerfulness and buoyancy of spirit so necessary for growth in holiness. Never let us forget that both convictions and consolations alike come from Him Who loves us.—*Probe my wound, and also heal it, my Saviour and my God.*

April 20th.

Let us who live within the sound of the Gospel—who are accustomed to dwell upon its precious promises ponder well this truth, that "there is no benefit to us by Christ without union with Him." Let us who have been joined to the Saviour use all available means for cementing our union with Him, seeking strength and refreshment in the Supper of the Lord, and in all holy exercises.—*Lord, make me Thine, not in name only, but really Thine.*

April 21st.

Do not let us regard the precepts of Holy Scripture as if they were too great for us to carry out in everyday life—too high for common practice. We may find it hard to live in obedience to them, but there they stand, and strive to rule our conduct by them we must.—*Teach me, divine Master, to obey not only in the letter, but in the spirit.*

April 22nd.

God has been very gracious in manifesting His Son to the world. In this country of ours, how many and how great are the manifestations of God's mercy and grace! What if we fall short of what is expected of us! To the believing, loving and obedient amongst us, He promises a special manifestation of Himself—an inward and spiritual manifestation.—*May the works of the Devil be destroyed in me—may God in Christ be revealed to me!*

April 23rd.

We are individuals, but we are also members of the Christian Church. We have religious duties to perform in common with other members of the Body of which Christ is the Head. However much time we may give to secret prayer, we must remember that no amount of private devotion exempts us from waiting upon God in His Sanctuary—from the duty of public worship.—*Lord, grant me by Thy Holy Spirit to have a right judgment in all things.*

April 24th.

Faith, truly so called, is far more than a mere theoretical belief, or assent to divine truth—it is an inward conviction which gradually sanctifies and purifies the heart; a mere acknowledgment of truth by the intellect has never made a man holier or purer. Is the heart to play no part in religion?—most certainly it must.—*Lord, give me such an intelligent perception and loving persuasion of Christian truth, as may influence my life.*

April 25th. (S. Mark.)

What, by the help of God, might we not accomplish, if we only made up our minds, and were thoroughly determined! We might meet with many a trial and many a difficulty—yes, and we might know many failures—but how much might be done! Might we not, after patient striving, have great cause for joy and thankfulness?—*Give me grace, Lord, to persevere, even amid discouragements, in all good works.*

April 26th.

One man may feel sorry for what he has done, because he fears that trouble will ensue upon his foolishness, or because he sees rocks ahead; another may feel vexed at having done a certain thing, because he is reaping present annoyance. The man of faith repents, and despairs not.—*Lord, grant that mine may be true repentance, not the remorse of Judas.*

April 27th.

It rests with the Christian to testify to his religion—to shew to all around what Christianity is. Never let us give any the impression that there is no difference between us and the world. When we mix in society let us guard the tongue, and shrink from every kind of evil. We need not immodestly force ourselves upon the notice of others, but we must never be ashamed to let our light shine.—*O Father, let me glorify Thee by Christian sincerity of life.*

April 28th.

Who would not wish to be a follower of Christ—to be like Him—to imitate Him? Even if the journey be difficult and the way hard, who would not wish to tread the same path which the Master trod? Those who are faithful to Christ here shall hereafter follow Him into glory, and even now their path shall be cheered and enlightened by Him. —*Lord Jesus, bid me come after Thee.*

April 29th.

Practice forgiveness—entertain no ill feelings towards another—look with compassion on the faults and shortcomings of others. Always be ready to overlook any wrong done by another on his repentance, then with confidence may you ask God for forgiveness on *your* repentance.— *O Father, forgive me all (forgiving others as I try to do) for the sake of Jesus Christ, Who died for me upon the Cross.*

April 30th.

I look around me in the world and see much which is discouraging and, seemingly, against me—I look above and see One Who loves me and cares for me, and I am comforted. Forsaken by some, opposed by others, laughed at by many, I thank God for any faithful friends He may have given me; yet I look above all else to Him.—*Reign in my heart, my King and my God.*

May 1st. (SS. Philip and James.)

The Saints of Scripture all point to the same Saviour. Though they possessed different gifts, and shewed differences of character, each having some prominent feature, they were all animated by the Holy Spirit of God. All men are more or less one-sided—the holiest are but fragments of the Master they follow. As Christians, we naturally love men in proportion as they put us in mind of Christ.—*Lord Jesus, make me more like Thyself.*

May 2nd.

How many there are who seem to live in a perpetual twilight, and to be quite satisfied that it should be so—all their belief is hazy and misty—there is no clearness about it—there is not that definite perception of truth which serves to make religion a personal thing—there is no taking home to themselves the precious promises of God! How is it with us?—*Lead, kindly Light—in Thy light shall I see light!*

May 3rd.

Prayers carefully said at fixed times tend to centre the mind on God, and to prevent an unsettled state of being, and that distraction and restlessness, so often produced by overmuch work, or excitement of any kind. They afford us a valuable antidote and help—only let them be of sufficient length (not to weary, but) to occupy the thoughts —to keep them in check—to give rest.—*Calm me, my God, and keep me calm.*

May 4th.

The Christian while on earth will ever know a state of mingled feelings—his joy will be tempered with sorrow, and his sorrow with joy. There will be much to make him glad, and yet, at the same time, he will find much to make him sad. He will be as one "sorrowful, yet alway rejoicing " —happy, if neither over-elated with joy, nor over-depressed with sorrow.—*Lord, make me quietly cheerful and contented.*

May 5th.

A lively Church Service does us good—our hearts go forth to God and to one another ; there is a lifting up of the countenance, and a lifting up of our whole being, when we sing the praises of God. We forget self—we learn to cast our cares, anxieties and troubles upon God—to shut out the cold, dark world—to look forward to Heaven's rest, and Heaven's eternal harmony.—*O Lord tune my heart, and open Thou my lips.*

May 6th.

Satan sometimes tempts us to look upon our corrupt nature as an excuse for sin—sometimes blinds our eyes to the truths of Scripture—sometimes lowers our view of holy ordinances, leading us to be inconstant at prayer, irregular in attendance at Church, thoughtless and inattentive when there. He will tempt us in the way in which we are most likely to fall.—*Make me, O God, wise and strong to resist the Tempter.*

May 7th.

How good it would be if we could see God's hand in all that befalls us—if we could thoroughly believe that God is dealing wisely with us—if we could know indeed that, in little things as well as in great, He is our divine Guide! What a comfort to feel that, after all, our lives are not a tangled skein!—*Make me, O Father, like Jesus my Saviour, trustful in my dependence on Thee.*

May 8th.

Think of God, and work as in His sight—a life of devotion, and of quiet activity and industry cannot go unblest. Upon the devout worker will come God's gift of peace. The Christian's life ought to be, like the life of Christ, full of inward peace—the Christian's prayers ought to be, like the prayers of Christ, full of calm and repose.—*Grant me, Lord, to live as in Thy presence—a life of prayer and active service.*

May 9th.

Our senses serve to connect us closely with the world in which we live, and we feel ourselves to be a part of it. How slow we are to learn of that life which can only be known through faith—how hard it is to separate ourselves (as it were) from the visible things around us—to these we cling! We realize in far too small a degree the spiritual and eternal.—*Teach me, O God, to walk by faith, and not by sight.*

May 10th.

How many are the ways in which we may acknowledge ourselves as the keepers of our brethren! God has willed that we should live together and be helpful to one another —that we should shew sympathy and love to all. We must examine ourselves and see how we, who are children of one Father, are doing our part as brethren—as members of one family—one Church.—*Save me, good Lord, from being selfish.*

May 11th.

Honesty and earnestness of purpose are not only required for what we call business, but also for gaining a knowledge of the truth, and for progress in the spiritual life. Religious knowledge does not come, as a matter of course, without trouble. Christian progress is not made without exertion. What a contrast is there between the pursuit of things of this world, and the pursuit of truth and holiness!—*Give me, Lord, the honest and good heart.*

May 12th.

In the family of God, each has his duties to perform, and each is indebted in some way to each. We must be careful to act aright towards all those amongst whom, in the providence of God, we find ourselves placed. Oh, that we might live together as members one of another, helping and serving one another—suffering and rejoicing together! —*Pardon, O Lord, my want of love in the past, and make me a better Christian.*

May 13th.

Call to mind the well-known picture of a boy with slate in hand poring over a sum which he finds difficulty in mastering. Is not that a faithful representation of many a child of man knitting his brow over profit and loss in the business world? Remove that calculation into another sphere, and work it out if you will—" What shall it profit a man, if he gain the whole world, and lose his own soul ? " —*Make me wise-hearted, O Lord.*

May 14th.

How many there are who do not seem to look upon almsgiving as a duty owed to God and to their fellow-men ! Some of us may be hindered from being outwardly as charitable as we would wish, from causes of which the outside world is not aware, but, before we are content with what we are already doing, let us each ask the question as in the presence of God—Can I do more ?—*From all selfishness, good Lord, deliver me.*

May 15th.

We all meet with disappointments, but this life of ours is not *all* disappointment. It disappoints those who look to it as being able to supply all their wishes—to fulfil all their longings, but not in the same way those who, understanding its purpose, are looking for something beyond it. The day will come to the believer in the Crucified One, when life's disappointments shall be over, and life's expectations shall be realized.—*Grant, Lord, that I may find mercy in that day.*

May 16th.

Kindness to men in their temporal necessities is the handmaid of Christianity. Practical sympathy most can appreciate- it appeals to men. There are different ways of shewing kindliness in the world—the manifestations of the sweetness of Christianity will differ according to circumstances; all may advance Christianity by, in some way, commending it to the favourable notice of others.—*Lord, make me a useful missionary in my home, and round about my home.*

May 17th.

We must look not only to the effect of our conduct upon ourselves, but to the influence which it may have upon those who come frequently across our path—our friends and neighbours. It is a very worldly saying which tells us never to mind what people say. The opinion of others may matter little to *us*, but to *others* the judgment which they form of us may be important.—*Save me, O God, from causing others to stumble.*

May 18th.

Let us beware of neglecting to use opportunities of getting spiritual strength. A time may await us which may put us to the test—we may be overtaken in a fault— we may be taken by surprise; we must prepare for whatever may betide. If we would be ready to meet temptation, we must have our armour on.—*Grant, Lord, that I may be girded with strength for the battle.*

May 19th.

The sacrifice of Christ for the sins of the world, proclaiming the love of God to the sinner, at the same time makes protest against sin. The Cross is at once the measure of God's love and of man's sin, and manifests God's hatred of sin and love to the sinner. We must fight against the sins which caused the Saviour to suffer, if we would have part in His victory.—*May the love of Christ constrain me!*

May 20th.

We must not tear away passages of Scripture from other passages which may serve to explain them. By doing so, we shall often have but one side of a truth, left without the balance of a counter-truth—heresies are often one-sided truths, rent away from the great body of the truth. We never need be afraid of statements made in God's Holy Word, but, from the various parts of inspired Scripture, we must gather truths, and learn the whole truth by comparing one passage with another.—*O God, teach me.*

May 21st.

Circumstances are often complained of when men should blame themselves, for the circumstances of life are to us very much what we make them—men complain of them much in the same way as bad workmen complain of their tools. Be sure they are designed for our good—let us use them aright.—*Lord, be Thou my Guard and Guide.*

May 22nd.

Straightforwardness of character is much to be desired among men, and where found is much to be admired, and much to be valued. Frankness, saying what we mean, and meaning what we say, ought to be cultivated by all. We should try to be sincere in every way. Alas, how many are wanting in sincerity and truthfulness!—*Holy Spirit of truth and love, teach and enable me to speak the truth in love—plain, sober words of truth.*

May 23rd.

As born in a Christian land, of Christian parents—as baptized into the Church of Christ, we have been undoubtedly called of God. Looking back through life, may we not see that all along God has been calling us—guiding us, and, in spite of our wanderings, the coldness of our love, following us with messages of truth and peace—working all things together in marvellous ways, intending our good? —*O God, grant that I may not resist Thee.*

May 24th.

Faith in Christ, and the practice of good for His sake, will form a bond of union which nothing shall be able to break. Other things may bring men together, but religion alone will bind men together; men may seem to be united by other means, but to be truly united men must be spiritually united.—*O Holy Spirit of God, teach me the meaning of those words of inspiration so often read—in Christ—in Him.*

May 25th.

How good to realize God's presence! The act of cruelty or unkindness—the act of dishonesty—the pleasant act of sin could not be done by us, if we were convinced that the eye of a loving Father was upon us. The word idly or rashly spoken would be silenced—the temper uncontrolled—the temper planning revenge could not find place. Thought, word, and deed would be influenced by the realization of God's presence.—*O God, shew me Thyself.*

May 26th.

Is it not a privilege to have in our midst an open Church to which we are invited?—we should value our Christian privileges. The Church bell is continually reminding us of prayer—the reading of God's Word—Christian teaching—the service of thanksgiving and praise—Holy Communion. Oh, that we might love to wait upon God, in Christ-appointed ways, quickened by His Holy Spirit!—*Make me glad, O Lord, to go to Thy House.*

May 27th.

Oh, that within our homes there might be that love which thinks, speaks, and acts after the manner of Christ—that forbearance which is so necessary—that gentleness and goodness and meekness which belong to the Christian character—that fidelity without which we cannot live and work happily together—that purity which clears the eyes to see God—that joy which the worldly never know—that peace which comes from above !—*Grant me, Lord, the fruits of Thy Holy Spirit.*

May 28th.

During the time that the Incarnate Son dwelt among us, He lived in time, and He lived in space—He was subject to the laws of our nature, could only be in one place at a time; but on His Ascension all was changed. His presence is no longer confined to any one part of the earth. He is the great King of all the earth, always with His praying people everywhere.—*Lord Jesus, abide with me.*

May 29th.

Are our hearts set upon present enjoyment, or upon future blessedness? Some speak as if acting with a view to future reward were selfishness—surely this is not so. The Lord Jesus set a bright future before men, to discourage them from sin. Duty and real self-interest, indeed, are one, but to deny oneself in order to be a true Christian cannot be selfishness.—*Guide me, good Lord, so shall I walk aright.*

May 30th.

What a blessing it is to have a Bible so cheap and so well translated! How many opportunities we have of acquiring knowledge and understanding of Holy Scripture! Do we profit by our advantages, and make use of our privileges? What a shame if we should be little better than those to whom the Bible has been a closed, or a mutilated Book !—*Make me anxious, O God, to learn Thy truth.*

May 31st.

The continual repetition of any form of words, or any set of truths, in which we shew ourselves to have no concern, and no real interest, will produce the same effect upon us as our familiarity with sounds is known to do. The ticking of a clock or watch may at first serve to disturb our rest, growing familiar with the sound we no longer hear it nor are interrupted by it.—*Lord, give me such a lively interest in the Services of Thy House, that frequency of repetition may add strength to my devotion.*

June 1st.

Do we *love* the truth? Do we *live* the truth? Are we walking in the presence of the Eternal One—are we being led closer and closer to the Saviour of mankind? These are not commonplace questions, but questions of the highest importance. Whatever we may know of the truth, let us be thankful ; never lose sight of it, but follow on to know more.—*Grant me, Lord, in this life knowledge of Thy truth, and hereafter life eternal.*

June 2nd.

We do not know what the future will be—we will be given to present effort, hoping all things. God, in His love, hides the future from us. He would have us to be active, painstaking and persevering with regard to our present duties—to wait in humble dependence upon Him, to be led on to better things ; and, when this life is over, to be called up higher.—*Grant, Lord, that I may be intent on pleasing Thee.*

June 3rd.

There is no room for despondency in the Christian life, but much need of redoubled energy. We want bright hope to spur us onwards. It is not enough for us to mean well—wish well—resolve well, but we must strive—strain every nerve—concentrate all our efforts. Let there be no mistake about our endeavours to take the Kingdom with a quiet enthusiasm, and by a holy violence.—*Bid me, O Lord, be brave and enduring.*

June 4th.

Where is the true fear of God?—where is the real hatred of sin?—where the holy indignation at wrong-doing?—where the sincere love of the truth? The practice of professing Christians speaks to us of a great deal of lukewarmness. Instead of forming a mere opinion of what religion ought to be, we ought to learn from Scripture in what it really consists.—*Help me, O my God, to live the life of godliness.*

June 5th.

We must try to live the life of faith—the devotional use of the Bible, reverent and habitual prayer will help us much. We must do our best to imitate those who set us a good example. How often do steady application to work—earnest perseverance in well-doing—patience under affliction—submission under suffering speak to us of an inner life which is not of earth, but of Heaven!—*Grant, O Lord, that I may be reckoned among Thy faithful ones.*

June 6th.

The children of the world seem sometimes to have the advantage over Christians in this life. The true follower of Christ, however, though he has his peculiar sorrows, has also his peculiar joys, while the triumphs of the worldly-minded are not what they seem. Some are cheerful for a time because they are thoughtless. The believer has a depth of peace, and freedom from care, unknown to others. —*Give me, Lord, real gladness of heart.*

June 7th.

Whatever our employment may be, we must try to bear witness, by the very manner and way in which we set about it, that we seek something above and beyond it. The Christian suffers not the things which are seen to have an undue influence over his conduct—having a firm conviction of the realities of the unseen and eternal, he lives a life of faith.—*O God, bid me look up to Thee—lift up my heart to Thee.*

June 8th.

How often the young spurn the advice given to them! How often those of riper years resent the being, as they think, dictated to! How much happier should we be, if we availed ourselves of the experience of others ; and how much wiser would it be for us to be willing to accept the counsel of those whose judgment is likely, for very obvious reasons, to be clearer than our own!—*Make me, Lord, more willing to be guided aright.*

June 9th.

Shall we not believe that God is with us in our everyday life ? Shall we not, each one of us, going about our daily task, be assured of God's watchful providence? What a comfort when we think of the risks, hazards, and dangers which beset us, to cast our cares upon God, knowing that He cares for us, and that we are in His keeping!—*Keep me, O God, for I trust in Thee.*

June 10th.

We ought to live thankful lives. We owe a debt of gratitude to God, the Giver of all good—the human heart should be alive to all benefits received at His hands. We ought to know something about the *sacrifices* of thanksgiving—the shewing forth of thankfulness to God, not only with our lips but in our lives—devoting ourselves increasingly to His service.—*Make use of me, O God.*

June 11th. (S. Barnabas.)

It is to a service of love we are called—the particular form which that service takes will differ according to gifts and circumstances, but all Christians are called to do service of some sort—we must never dare to say that we are off duty—is not Christ's yoke upon us ? When our hearts are set at liberty, we must run in the way of God's commandments.—*Make me happy, Lord, in working for Thee.*

June 12th.

Looking to Jesus, we may learn a lesson of faith, and a lesson of love. As man He never lost faith in His Heavenly Father—under all circumstances and at all times, the same faithful One; and love was ever ruling His whole life—self-denying love held Him to the Cross.—*Blessed Saviour, make me one of Thy faithful people, and grant that I may have a loving heart continually.*

June 13th.

There is one thing of supreme importance; even if all other things go wrong, and many discomforts attend your daily walk, remember, it is but for a time. How trifling and insignificant are the things of earth, which will one day be shaken and removed, when compared with the comforts and joys arising from a life of communion with God—eternal life!—*O God, teach me to see things in the real light—make me live.*

June 14th.

We live amongst our fellows—we live not alone—we have not only ourselves, but others to look to. We influence those amongst whom we live, as they also have an influence over us—man has a strange and wonderful influence over his brother-man, it is a fact which cannot be denied.—*O Father, overrule any bad influence which I have exerted in life, and make me henceforth an influence for good in the world.*

June 15th.

Live as the redeemed of God—look realities in the face—grasp the truth to which Jesus, the Son of God, bore witness in His life and by His death—measure all by the Redeemer's Cross—yourselves be real and true. Be not drawn away by the worldliness which reigns around—look above for protection, for guidance, and for power.—*Prosper me, O God, lead me on to better things, and prepare me for Thine eternal Kingdom.*

June 16th.

What a forcible sermon do the disappointments of life preach to us, they seem to say "seek those things which are above"! Let us accept the Holy Ghost as our Guide to lead our thoughts Heavenward, and to teach us not to despair, but, while we do our duty here, as well as we possibly can, cheerfully to live for the great Future to which Christ testified.—*Father, lift up the hearts of Thy children.*

June 17th.

We need to live somewhat by rule, and to be strict with ourselves, constantly throwing ourselves into an attitude of devotion. The outward ordinances of the Church, cold and lifeless as they may appear to some, are health-giving to those who use them aright. Forms used systematically, earnestly, and dutifully, cannot but tend to mould the character, and to help forward the spiritual life.—*Grant, O God, that I may never, through carelessly using the means, lose Thy blessing.*

June 18th.

The Christian ought to speak out his mind, in word and in action, and to shew that he is ready to stand his ground, and maintain the cause of right and truth—he ought to be most careful to avoid laying himself open to the charge of inconsistency in any way; even little inconsistencies will prove great hindrances to the cause of Christ, and bring discredit upon religion.—*Teach me, O Heavenly Father, to walk carefully before Thee.*

June 19th.

It is the having untrue and unworthy ideas of God, not the thought that God is a forgiving God, which makes us careless and unsteady. Faith in God's forgiving spirit has a tendency to make us better, holier, and purer. Firm belief in God's readiness to forgive the sins of which we repent, will make us anxious to please Him.—*Grant, Lord, that, trusting in Thy mercy, I may love and fear Thee, and walk uprightly in Thy sight.*

June 20th.

It may be we are anxious to feel ourselves, and to be thought to be, on the side of Christ; but what room is there for advancement in the spiritual life! When aroused to better things we must take care not to cool down, and lose holy energy and zeal. It is not enough to be just within sight of the Saviour—to follow Him afar off—we must press on into His presence.—*Holy Spirit, be my strength and guide.*

June 21st.

Our Heavenly Father wishes to see us happy, but He knows that before we can be happy we must be striving after holiness, and before this, too, there must be a knowledge of sin. When we realize our sinfulness, we betake ourselves to the Saviour, and look for the Holy Spirit's help. Knowing our disease and seeking its cure we shall be happy; but not so, living on in ignorance and blindness. —*Lead me, O Father, in the right way.*

June 22nd.

What would the world in its social state have been without Christ? All that distinguishes Christendom from Heathendom has its starting point in Him—nothing else could have produced fruits like His life. The love of Christ has constrained men to be kind—Hospitals, Homes, Refuges have sprung from Him, the good Physician - the binder-up of the broken limbs of humanity.—*Lord, make me zealous in good works, shed Thy love abroad in my heart.*

June 23rd.

Christianity does not concern itself merely with externals—it penetrates far deeper than the surface; it does not concern itself with the mere outward fashion—it goes to the heart of the matter, a fair outside will not do. Gospel-holiness requires that there should be purity *within.*
— "*Create in me a clean heart, O God, and renew a right spirit within me.*"

June 24th. (S. John Baptist.)

It is no good to sit down and mourn over the sinful state of the world—it is for us, asking God's blessing, to be up and in action. Cannot evils be redressed? Is the Lord's arm shortened? Cannot all who have felt the preciousness of truth do something for others? Say—By God's help, I will do my best. Pray—*Lord, shew me what I may do for Thee, and bless the work of all true labourers.*

June 25th.

Sometimes we may calculate on a man being honest from reasons of prudence, when we could not count on his honesty of principle—but one who is honest because he finds it the best policy is not the truly honest man. Be truly honest in little things as well as in great—how often do the little things of life shew what a man is!—*O God, make me real, true and upright—correct in me all crooked ways.*

June 26th.

Boldness of access is the privilege of one who knows that he has a reconciled Father, but irreverence is the characteristic of one who does not consider the majesty of God. We must draw near, with due and becoming reverence and godly fear, in full assurance of faith.—*Heavenly Lord, teach me to worship Thee aright.*

June 27th.

Entertain a loving spirit towards others—do not dwell upon their faults, but call their good qualities to mind. Bear a good will towards all. Have plenty of sympathy. Love knits men together in a holy fellowship—we cannot hurt those whom we love; and not only wish others well, but be practically kind, as often as possible.—*Lord Jesus, Who went about doing good, make me more and more like Thyself.*

June 28th.

In prayer the child tells his Father what his wishes are. Every prayer offered up in a true spirit will meet with a fitting answer. If *our* will be not the same as the will of God, and our request cannot be granted, then, if we have prayed aright, our crooked wills shall be straightened, and we shall be enabled, by inward light and strength given to us, to agree in the perfect will of God.—*Lord, teach me to pray.*

June 29th. (S. Peter.)

Who will be Christ's fishers?—who will do great and noble work for Him? How few there ever seem really anxious to do good in the world! We have not merely to be thinking of our own souls, but of the souls of others also. Have we no wish to catch others for Christ?—Is He never to say to us " Bring of the fish which ye have caught "?—*Lord, make me useful in Thy service.*

June 30th.

Though each one has his own burden to bear, we may help one another by our prayers. What comfort would it give to each one of us to know that we were being remembered and mentioned in the prayers of others!—*O Father, make us to see how we belong to one great family—how much we have in common—and how good is intercessory prayer.*

July 1st.

Duty! Privilege! How often we fail in doing the one—how often we fail in realizing the other! Our duty is to live *to* God—our privilege to live *with* God. Are we making way onwards and upwards to the Home which our Father has for us—which the Lord Jesus has gone before to prepare—whither the Holy Spirit is desirous to guide us, if we will only yield our wills to Him?—*Guide me, Lord, and bless me.*

July 2nd.

We must, when we go to Church, make up our minds to do real business with God ; we must think of what is taught us, determined to reduce what we learn to practice. Is there communion between the Spirit of God and our spirits—do we profit by what we hear—are we learning in our lives, as well as with our lips, to shew forth God's praise ?—*Good Lord, make my religion very real.*

July 3rd.

Do our Sundays and week-days harmonize ?—do we draw any improper distinction between the secular and the religious? Let us see to it. Our duties as citizens, and our duties as Churchmen are at one—work and worship make up life, and as ours is divine worship, so ours ought to be divine work—we cannot tear ourselves in two —*Teach me, good Lord, to be consistent.*

July 4th.

It is possible to maintain the thought of God throughout a busy life ; and not only possible, but most needful for the right discharge of duty—our work may be hallowed by frequent devotion, and the presence of God may be realized. The Christian does not make the less good workman. We must ever remember that we are the servants of God, and, as such, be continually witnessing to the good and true.— *Make me, O God, to see and serve Thee in all.*

July 5th.

Underlying all active service there must be a spirit of devotion—we must remember this If there is to be the useful life—if there is to be the life pleasing to God, beneath all there must be true, hearty devotion ; intercourse with God must be sustained—supplies of divine grace must be continually repairing all waste, and affording new strength. —*O God, Thou source of all good, support and further me in all good works.*

July 6th.

It is far easier to pull down than to build up—how many choose the easier task! This holds good in every department of life—it is often so in matters of religion. The Devil's work is the work of unsettling, spoiling, destroying, shaking in the faith, and bringing to ruin. God would have us attend to the work of edifying—the building up of ourselves and others in our most holy Faith. —*Strengthen me, O God, and settle me in Thy truth.*

July 7th.

Never let us forget the eternal Spirit—do not let us talk of human power and strength, or think of the world's machinery and human systems, forgetting the one great Spirit upon Whom all depends. How needful it is that our lives should be lives of prayerful dependence, and all our efforts trustfully made in reliance upon that divine help which is promised to those who seek!—*O God, by Thy Holy Spirit, be near me to guide and bless.*

July 8th.

Do we live in evil days—when have not the days been evil? Perhaps some ages have seen darker days than others. We need not speak disparagingly of our own times; we have, however, our special dangers to contend with—we must be alive to these—fight against them—oppose them with a will, resolved to get the better of them, and to triumph by divine grace in spite of circumstances.—*Teach me, Lord God, to be prudent and circumspect.*

July 9th.

Do we ever think of the Church of Christ after a worldly fashion as a mere human institution—ignoring the work of the Holy Spirit in it, its Heart, its Life, its Guide—instead of a divine one, formed by the Christ of God, made to live by the life-giving Spirit—a divine institution, through which the Spirit works, calling us to holiness, and helping us to be holy?—*Grant, Lord Jesus, that I may be a living member of Thy Church.*

July 10th.

The Word of God taking upon Him our flesh not only has taught us of the Father of all in Heaven, but also has taught us (as a consequence) that we are brethren—bound together by a common humanity; He has revealed to us, moreover, a higher and better brotherhood—a Christian brotherhood. Christ, by uniting the human and the divine, has taught us to love both God and man.—*Pour into my heart, O God, the most excellent gift of love.*

July 11th.

We must bring our offering in a clean vessel into the House of the Lord—we must not think that we can compensate for personal holiness by a little liberality. Almsgiving is right and proper, but God asks us to give ourselves to Him—we must not forget the duty of self-dedication—giving ourselves to the Lord. Our gifts offered in Christ's name will be accepted for His sake.—*O God, make me grow both in kindness and in holiness.*

July 12th.

Unchristian tempers sorely hinder the real work of the Church. There *are* conditions under which, it would seem, we cannot expect the blessing of God. Christians must try to draw nearer together—to understand one another better—to put themselves in a proper attitude for receiving divine favour. Oh, that we had more Christianity in our hearts!—we should work more prosperously, and with more fulness of blessing.—*Enable us, good Lord, to work together for Thy glory.*

July 13th.

Life to the Christian is a continual coming to Christ—it must be so. Whether coming for the first time, or coming as we have often come before, seeking again and again more earnestly to come, we come by *loving*. With thanksgiving and praise—with prayer and holy effort let us faint not, but persevere—our course is onward and upward —Christ-ward—it is a journey of love.—*O make me love Thee more and more!*

July 14th.

Intercession is a Christian duty, and a Christian privilege; we must plead for others before the throne of grace, not, indeed, in a spirit of self-sufficiency, but of profound humility—in all lowliness—with a deep sense of our own dependence upon God— yearning ourselves for a closer walk with Him. For whom do we pray? We must offer our intercessions through the mediation of our great Intercessor in Heaven.—*Teach me, Lord Jesus, to pray for others—individually as well as collectively.*

July 15th.

Familiarity with the whole of the Bible is most desirable—happy they who acquire it in the days of childhood and youth! As we go on in life, if we be diligent seekers, the Bible will be continually opening up to us new treasures—treasures brought to light from beneath its surface will be hailed with joy; we shall find how inexhaustible is our Bible-store.—*O God, make me glad of Thy Word.*

July 16th.

The Christian is called to live above the world. We must be thankful, indeed, for all the blessings we have *now* to enjoy, but life *here* is only for "a little while." We must look upon all as lent us by God, and never lose sight of the Giver—while we use God's gifts we must see Him in all, and when He bids us we must be ready to give up all.—*Grant me, Lord, an eternity of bliss.*

July 17th.

Good will it be for us, if experience should teach us how dependent we are upon the grace of God—how foolish it is to be too self-reliant, and to think ourselves strong. If wise, we shall keep out of harm's way—out of the way of temptation, we shall not dally with sin. Clothed with humility we will try to learn what it is to "pray without ceasing."—*Lord, keep me humble, and make me "bold in self-despair."*

July 18th.

If we would make progress in the Christian life, we must be daily asking ourselves questions in the way of self-examination, and, confessing our sins and faults, seek pardon from God; we must, too, ask God for grace to overcome evil and to do right, and determine to live, not leaning upon any arm of flesh, but upon His strong arm—each day is a life in miniature.—*Pardon, O God, for the past, and grace for the future !*

July 19th.

It is difficult to attain to self-knowledge—we can see the faults of others much more clearly than our own—we see the mistakes which others make, but we easily deceive ourselves. God can reveal us to ourselves—teach us to know ourselves. Humility will follow upon true self-knowledge, and it is very necessary that we should be humble, if we would be students in the school of Christ.—*Teach me, my Master, the lessons I most need to learn.*

July 20th.

That which you are convinced is right, do. Never mind the frowns or smiles of the world, for you will have to stand before a higher than any earthly tribunal. Never be frightened from your allegiance to Christ—shew a zeal which has no foolish reasonings or questionings—shew fulness of purpose, Christian determination to stand humbly, yet fearlessly, at the post of duty.—*Strengthen me, O Lord, with the Holy Ghost the Comforter.*

July 21st.

Much of the work that we have to do in this world is in the way of remedying the evils we find within us and around us—to remedy evil already done is a very true part of Christian work. Let us prevent what we can; and what has not been prevented, let us seek to cure—let us seek to repair the ills of the past.—*Make me wise, O God, to act.*

July 22nd.

It is a very blessed thing to feel warm in one's love to God—then, if I have sinned, I go at once and ask for forgiveness; if I want comfort, strength, consolation, I know where to seek it and to find it—I go to God as a child to a Father—I go to Him to tell Him of my sorrows, and to tell Him of my joys.—*Bid me draw near, O Lord, in full assurance of faith.*

July 23rd.

God's glory!—let this be our aim—let this give a singleness and simplicity to our lives—let this make duty easy and pleasant. We must seek to glorify God in our worldly calling—in our everyday life. Away then with low aims—with minding earthly things—with all self-seeking—seeking our own glory! How much of what we do points Heavenward?—*Save me and deliver me, O God, from all selfishness and worldliness.*

July 24th.

That form of teaching which deals with our Lord simply as a man—a great, good, and noble man—is very fascinating; but we must ever remember that this is only a one-sided view to take. We must not separate what God has joined together—the man is also God, our Saviour and Redeemer—the channel of all grace for the purifying of our fallen nature, and for the perfecting of the new creature. —*Teach me, blessed Jesus, to call Thee " my Lord and my God."*

July 25th. (S. James.)

It is good to observe Saints' Days. By so doing we shew our appreciation of lives rightly spent, and bear witness before the world by paying reverence to the good and the true. At the same time we are encouraged by the examples of those whom we commemorate, and are led to seek for ourselves the grace of God which made them what they were.—*Make me to be " numbered with Thy Saints in glory everlasting."*

July 26th.

We must not confound the means of grace with grace itself—with the end to which they serve. It is by a right use of ordinances that we hope to be enabled to live the life of godliness—to live near to God when occupied with our daily tasks—to walk with God in daily life when doing the work of life's calling.—*Give me, Lord, a good understanding in the ways of godliness.*

July 27th.

It might be thought that to have our sins always before us would produce such a sorrowful spirit, that we should never be able to go through life with anything of cheerfulness. Christian sorrow, however, resulting from a right view of the nature of sin, should not incapacitate us for work, but urge us on and further us, who know there is a remedy, in the spiritual life.—*Grant, Lord, that, with faith in my Saviour, I may never despair.*

July 28th.

Do we not often feel in need of stirring up and arousing? Have we not often borne in upon us our need of holiness? Oh, that our spiritual life might be deepened—that our faith might be stronger—that our hope might be brighter—that our love might be more real—our sense of duty more sustained—our lives more of a piece and more consistent—that we might be more true to our Christian name!—*Lord, suffer me not to faint.*

July 29th.

We read in Holy Scripture of the armour of righteousness—the armour of light—the armour of God. Good would it be for us to wear this armour—it would save us from many an evil; but there is another armour which we are wont to put on, we are prone to encase ourselves in self-righteousness—this renders us proof against all spiritual good.—*Teach me, O God, that all merit is in Jesus.*

July 30th.

We are in motion forwards or backwards—ours is either progression or retrogression—there is no such thing as stagnation in the spiritual life. Our love of God and delight in His service is either becoming greater or growing less. However it may have been in the past, our watchword for the future must be *forward*—we must go forward with faith and hope in God.—*Stir up my will, O God, and urge me on.*

July 31st.

We must be very humbly dependent upon God, as we seek to build up our spiritual life—to grow in holiness. God having taught us to know ourselves, we must seek His help to restrain and overcome our evil tendencies, and to foster and further any inclination to good that we may have. If He sees us given to real effort, God will work in us that which is well-pleasing to Him.—*Truly weak in myself, make me, O God, truly strong in Thee.*

August 1st.

The Gospel of Jesus Christ—the story of the Crucified One is the very antidote for human pride. A spirit of humility must pervade the Christian life, there must be a willingness to repose on the Saviour's merits—to work in His strength—to live by His life—to be saved by Him eternally. Let sinful self be abased, and the sinless Sin-bearer exalted.—*Be Thou my Jesus and my all!*

August 2nd.

Let us try to grasp the truth of our immortality. We see death ever to be busy around us, but supposing we have good hope of forgiveness—of the blotting out of our sins—why then, the sting is gone, and death is robbed of its terrors. In a sense, death will remain, but it can do us no harm—we feel that we shall be conquerors through Christ. —*Lord Jesus, receive my spirit, and grant me a happy resurrection.*

August 3rd.

Our religion must be a reality—we must not dwell in dreamland—we must have root in ourselves, and a reason for our hope. We must now and then put our religion to more than a usual test. Are we conquering sin—becoming more strictly obedient—making true headway—really growing Christ-like in character and life, in thought, word, and deed?—*O God, make me real and true, genuine in devotion, and thorough in work.*

August 4th.

In this world, where all things are double, we are trained, by the use of earthly relationships and ties, to look above and note their heavenly patterns—the great realities of which they are the shadows. Are we being led on from the earthly to the Heavenly—from the natural to the spiritual? Is the home on earth fitting us for the Home in Heaven?—*Teach me, O God, to use types and emblems to my eternal profit.*

August 5th.

Life is a little span in which we may do something for the glory of God, and for the benefit of our fellow-creatures. It is for us to work while we have opportunity—it is no good to delay—the time is short. We must not be discouraged because it seems that we can do but little—that should rather be an incentive to earnestness.—*Lord, make me to do what I can, diligently and well.*

August 6th.

Is not the Church of Christ an army—an exceeding great army? The Spirit of God animates men with the divine life, and, influenced by divine grace, they become soldiers marshalled under the banner of the Cross —devoted —obedient— well-disciplined—brave—enduring —fighting their way on to victory through Christ. How goes the fight? Have we good hope of triumph after battle.—*Breathe upon us, O Spirit of the living God, that we may live.*

August 7th.

We must be ruled not by our desires and inclinations, but by a sense of duty—we must know what it is to put a restraint upon ourselves—we must know what it is to exercise self-discipline. Our lives must not be unruly, but governed by Christian principles; it ought plainly to appear that Christ is our King, and that we are seeking to live in loving subjection to Him.—*Lord Jesus, reign within me.*

August 8th.

Our lots are variously cast—we have different advantages—how diverse are the lives of men! Sometimes those who seemingly have most against them succeed the best, while those who have very much in their favour fail most dreadfully. God is ready to make up all inequalities, so let none complain or make excuse—let none presume. Failure means our own fault—want of earnestness in seeking God's special grace.—*Grant, Lord, that I may ever lean humbly and trustfully on Thee.*

August 9th.

Do not the Psalms very often put into our mouths the very thoughts we would wish to utter—express our real desires? Sometimes, however, the Psalmist's words may seem to go beyond us—to be somewhat unreal upon our lips; shall we, in such case, leave off using them? No, we will use them as sincerely as we can—they may beget in us the yearning, the lack of which we deplore, stirring us up to nobler aspirations.—*Enlarge and ennoble, O Lord, my desires.*

August 10th.

There is a difference between offence given and offence taken—there is often a taking of offence when there really has been no giving of offence. We are far too apt to take offence. On the one hand we must be careful to have due respect for one another's feelings, and on the other hand we must not be too sensitive, and so make absurd martyrs of ourselves.—*Teach me, good Lord, to walk as a Christian among men.*

August 11th.

It is our duty so to live as Christians, that we may remind the world of God. While we do nothing for the sake of ostentation, or purposely to attract attention to ourselves, we must not seek to hide our Christianity in order to escape unpleasantness, but let it have free play. We must beware of moral cowardice—anything like a compromising spirit. Humbly and truthfully we must testify to Christ by word and deed.—*Make me, Lord Jesus, a witness for Thee.*

August 12th.

We have all of us cause to be thankful—may God spare us from the sin of ingratitude! Yet are there not some who feel but little true thankfulness? We should try to enter into each clause of our beautiful General Thanksgiving, and weave thanksgiving also into our private prayers. Alas, that we should ask for what we want, and forget to return thanks for the blessings which are daily granted!—*Impress me, O God, with a sense of all Thy mercies.*

August 13th.

Let us endeavour to grow more large-hearted, and to rise above that natural selfishness which intrudes even into our religion. Do not let us think of ourselves alone—of our salvation only. Let us think of the great work of redemption planned by the large, loving heart of God our Father, and let us work and pray—pray and work—for the gathering in of Christ's people from the whole world.—*Train my heart, O God, and enlarge it.*

August 14th.

There is danger in toleration—Christianity *does* teach charity, but does *not* teach a too lenient toleration. We must never forget that we are stewards of God, and have been intrusted with a holy deposit of truth—never let us be silent, while truth is being watered down—never let us seem to acquiesce in any unholy compromise, shewing a time-serving, men-pleasing spirit.—*O God, make me a lover of Thy truth.*

August 15th.

We cannot acquire holiness by any course of discipline, however severe and rigorous, without God's grace given to us through Christ, the Incarnate Son. We need God to work and live within us. We talk about human effort; this must be made, it is true, but there must be a giving up of ourselves to God, that He may work in us—we cannot live independently of God.—*Grant, O God, that I may yield myself to Thee.*

August 16th.

Christ bore His Cross, the Christian must not murmur if he has a cross to bear—why not take it up! It may be we are often tempted to shirk unpleasant duties, and to refrain from speaking unpleasant words; it may be we are often tempted to please ourselves or others at the cost of Christian principle, but we must remember Christ pleased not Himself, and His duty to His Heavenly Father was ever before Him.—*Lord Jesus, strengthen me.*

August 17th.

Faith is in the spiritual life what sense is in the natural life—hence faith is called the eye of the soul. It is not enough that God's eye be fixed on us, our eye must be fixed on God. We must not only know that God's eye is upon us, but we ourselves must try to catch God's eye; then we shall be happy—assured of loving protection and guidance.—*Lord, I look to Thee, undertake for me.*

August 18th.

Some persons are very difficult to understand. We cannot with equal ease read all alike, but we have not, generally, to be for long together in the society of any, without discovering what it is they reckon of supreme importance. A keen observer of human nature can read characters with a tolerable degree of accuracy; wealth—learning—accomplishments—position—strength—beauty—self-righteousness—all these are gloried in—ah, some glory in their shame!—*Make me, Lord Jesus, to glory in Thy Cross.*

August 19th.

What are we doing that shews that we love our neighbours—is ours practical love? Good feelings merely will not do—impulse only will not do; we must act, and that, too, on steady, abiding, Christian principle, which shall not pass quickly away, or live only by fits and starts, but shall endure—shall remain. Love to others is a test of our religion.—*Teach me, Lord Jesus, to be truly kind and loving.*

August 20th.

God asks of us obedience and submission to His will, but, before granting His request, we need, perhaps, to know Him better than we do. Oh, that we might know Him and trust in Him as our Father!—oh, for a devoted, cheerful will to please Him as such!—oh, that we might lovingly say, "Our Father, Thy will be done" *in* us and *by* us, and feel and mean what we say!—*God, grant that I may love and serve Thee.*

August 21st.

We may test the character of our devotions by the influence which they have upon our lives—in what way are we the better for them? Oh, that we might so profit by religious exercises that we might be wise and strong to regulate our daily life aright, and to perform our duties as those who, having been with Jesus, have learnt, indeed, the meaning of the old, old story, and love it well!—*Give me grace, Lord, for active service.*

August 22nd.

We believe in a living Christ. The ministry which the Lord Jesus carried on when on earth, He continues by His Spirit—His work is now even greater and more extended. Christ is with His people—our privileges, as Christians, are such that we can speak to Him when we will, without any diffidence, or shyness, or reserve—there is no waiting for an opportunity—we can always bring ourselves into His presence.—*Lord, make me both earnest and thankful.*

August 23rd.

Can we not remember times when the Holy Spirit of God has striven with us, and we have been stubborn and self-willed—when thinking ourselves to be in the right, we have blinded our eyes to the possibility of our being in the wrong—when we have been warned, and yet in vain—when circumstances have seemed to have a voice for us, and we have not heeded it?—*Speak, Lord, for Thy servant heareth.*

August 24th. (S. Bartholomew.)

We must pray for our own families—much of our own happiness being closely mixed up with them, let us beware of selfishness ; for the holy work going on in our own beloved Church and Country—but even Christendom must not be the limits of our intercession ; we must pray for God's world, and especially for the missionary work of the Church in our Colonies and amongst the Heathen. Even the little ones of earth may do great things.— *Make me value, Lord, the quiet times of prayer.*

August 25th.

A voice comes from the Cross of Christ speaking of pardon and peace—it is the voice of Jesus the Crucified ; but I know that pardon and peace will not be mine unconditionally—I am called to a life of holiness. The voice from Calvary speaks of God's love, but also of condemnation to the sinner who will not repent—"Take heed how ye hear."—*Give me, Lord, the hearing ear, and the understanding heart.*

August 26th.

It will never do for us to be trying to serve God a little, and the world a little too. Singleness of heart is much to be prayed for—much to be sought for. God wants the love of our hearts. Oh, that we might be so filled with a desire to please God, that He might become the centre of all our thoughts, and all our energies—the very centre of our being !—*Deliver me, good Lord, from all double-mindedness.*

August 27th.

We must not be distracted by the things of this life, knowing that there is *one* thing of supreme concern—all else belongs to the things which shall one day pass away. Never let us neglect our eternal welfare—whatever else has to give way, *that* must have our attention. After death comes judgment—we have souls to save—we have to live for ever.—*Grant me, Lord, daily to seek and set my affection on things above.*

August 28th.

We want praying people, and we want working people in the Church—prayer and work must go together. We cannot expect the divine blessing unless we look up to God, and use, at the same time, our own efforts. Those who cannot possibly do active work for Christ can pray; but those must pray also who can and do work. There is no one who cannot do something for the Redeemer's Kingdom. —*Teach me, Lord, to fill my place aright.*

August 29th.

At one time we are too severe, and at another too lax. To regulate our conduct aright, we should mark well the Lord Jesus. See, He hates sin and loves the sinner—He looks upon sin as a reality—He looks upon the weakness of man as a reality—He looks upon human effort as a reality—He looks upon divine grace as a reality.—*O God, make me Christ-like in my thoughts, and in my dealings.*

August 30th.

Just as in a school there can be no proper teaching unless there is good order, so, as long as there is disorder and confusion in our inner life, there can be no true advance. For progress in the spiritual life there must be peace and quietness within, whatever may be our outward circumstances. Do we know the blessings of inward repose, so essential to our religious well-being?—*Speak peace, Lord, to my soul.*

August 31st.

Remember, kindness shewn to the needy—help given to those who want it is pleasing in the sight of Him Who loved us and gave Himself for us; Jesus our Lord counts it as shown to Himself, for He holds Himself to be one with His people. In the Bible you will find few rules to follow in the letter, but you will find the holy principles of the law of kindness throughout.—*What, dear Lord, can I do for Thee?*

September 1st.

We live here on earth, and so did the Lord Jesus for awhile. He was both God and Man—the God-Man. Christ connects us with Heaven—in Him is stored up all that we need for the quickening and growth of our spiritual life—Christ *in us* is our life—we live in Him. In Him Who stooped to earth we, if believing, shall be raised to Heaven.—*Lord, make me Thine, and Thine for ever.*

September 2nd.

What does God mean by His long-suffering and forbearance? Does He mean that He is indifferent to the wickedness that there is in the world? Is He indifferent to idle and sinful words, and cruel, unjust, and wrongful acts? No, indeed, a thousand times no; He is provoked every day—He will visit for these things—He is only keeping silence—He is patient—He waits to be gracious.—*Grant, Lord, that I may be found amongst Thy waiting ones.*

September 3rd.

What a dreadful thing it is to be suspicious, to feel in ourselves an absence of love and trust!—what a dreadful thing to feel that we are suspected—unloved—distrusted! Is there not need that we should do our best to draw together, acting kindly towards one another—not upbraiding, but speaking gently to one another's hearts, and proving real helps to one another in life's journey?—*Teach me, Lord, what that Scripture means—" none of us liveth to himself."*

September 4th.

Are we striving to serve God in all things—have we determined within ourselves to obey God, come what may—have we made up our minds, seeing the wretchedness of half-obedience, to give Him, as far as possible, the full measure of obedience—ever listening for His voice—ever ready to act upon any indication of His will—ever anxious to please Him ?—*Make me, good Lord, resolved what to do.*

September 5th.

We who live together on earth have a wonderful influence over one another—acting and re-acting upon one another. Let us think of this, that our lives may be for good. How careful should we be with regard to all our words and actions, knowing that what we do and say may exercise some subtle influence over others! Influence is a talent for which the Master will hold us responsible.—*Bless me, O my Father, and make me a blessing.*

September 6th.

Let us know this, that we have a Father in Heaven Who is loving and kind, as well as just and true, and that though an earthly father might meet a once disobedient child with the words " you are no child of mine," our Heavenly Father is ever ready to welcome the returning one. Never let us drop that sweet name " Father "—it makes the humble bold—it makes duty a pleasure.—*O God, give me right thoughts of Thee.*

September 7th.

There are various ways in which we may shew forth our love to God—love is multiform in its manifestations; but no surer token of love and affection can be given than the constantly coming and laying bare our hearts before Him with their joys and their sorrows, their yearnings and their fears—it is the simple and sincere way of a child—it is the very language of childlike sincerity and simplicity.—*O God, that I may love Thee more and more!*

September 8th.

Can you believe that Christ's service is pleasant ?—no one can compel you to believe it, nor prove it to you; but if you will act and put it to the test, you will find out for yourself that it is so. How many, who have begun with trying and struggling, have ended with experiencing the pleasantness of duty—the happiness of doing God's service. —*Bid me, Lord Jesus, take up Thy easy yoke.*

September 9th.

Earthly tribunals concern themselves with the acts of men, but religion concerns itself with the heart. Human law only punishes where there is a discovery of guilt—only punishes the sinner who is found out; but God, unto whom all hearts are open, looks for truth, uprightness, and purity of heart—He knows, beyond all doubt, where to strike—where to spare.—*O God, incline my heart to keep Thy laws.*

September 10th.

Our spiritual life must be healthy. As to the way in which it is to be developed, much must be left to the individual. There are certain rules which can be laid down, but, as we are so differently constituted, there will ever be diversities of practice, within certain limits, to suit the individual. Religion must be a personal thing between us and God—holy intercourse with God.—*Bind me, O God, to Thee.*

September 11th.

We may say that there is but one work for man in life—the work of God. Each workman has his own proper place—some work has to do more particularly with things spiritual—some more particularly with things temporal. Should the spiritual worker neglect the temporal needs which come before Him—the worker in things temporal his opportunities for spiritual good, both alike will fail to imitate the Master.—*Grant, Lord, that I may work in a right spirit.*

September 12th.

It is true we do not live in days of rough and savage persecution, but nevertheless religion has its enemies—goodness will ever provoke the enmity of the wicked. If we suffer petty persecution, we must not complain—it is the lot of earnest Christians; we must not court it, but if we suffer it not in any degree, we may well question ourselves as to the reality of our religion.—*Make me, Lord, brave, humble, and cheerful, in bearing witness for Thee.*

September 13th.

Where is Christian self-denial—self-sacrifice? We see it around us, though not so generally as one would wish, but do we see it in ourselves? We are too prone to make religion easy. Do we give away anything but the superfluity of our money? Do we give ourselves up in any true sense to the Lord's work? The presence or absence of self-denial is a very real test to which we may bring ourselves.—*Help me, Lord Jesus, to follow Thee.*

September 14th.

Do we ever look upon the Lord Jesus Christ as one of whom we have read in history—with the events of whose life we are very familiar—whom we justly admire and would wish to imitate, and forget that He is a living Christ, and fail to ask the Holy Spirit to bring Him near to us—to fill us with life? If not anointed with divine power, how shall we grow like Him?—*Lord, give me life.*

September 15th.

Is there that brotherly trust and confidence among us which there ought to be? Is there not sometimes a shrinking from our fellows? If, on the one hand, there is too great carelessness about the feelings of others, is there not, on the other, too great readiness to be offended? Do not some think themselves injured before they are hurt, and speak as if every man were against them—or as if *few* were brothers?—*Save me, good Lord, from being unduly sensitive.*

September 16th.

Words of thanksgiving are more easily spoken than acts of thankfulness performed—we ought to see to it that we attend to the more difficult, as well as to the more easy. The outcome—the shewing forth of our thanks in acts may assume different forms—it is necessary that we should make some definite effort to acknowledge the good things which God has given us—the memorials of His abundant kindness.—*Teach me, Lord, in everything to give thanks.*

September 17th.

Are we growing holier?—if not, why not? Whose fault is it? Clearly our own. *God* does not fail in His promise to give the Holy Spirit to them that ask Him. *We* have failed to yield ourselves to God to work in us. Who is there who does not feel that man has the awful power of resisting, if he will, divine grace—grieving the Holy Spirit of God?—*Make me willing, O God, in the day of Thy power.*

September 18th.

Are we seeking God's blessing—are we preparing our hearts to receive it? The blessing is ready—are we ready and eager for it? We must empty our hearts of all that is sinful and worldly, remove all obstacles, and make room for what God is desirous to give us for His dear Son's sake. It is our own fault if we remain unblest, or receive not fulness of blessing.—*Make me anxious, Lord, to receive "the things of the Spirit."*

September 19th.

In proportion as we ourselves know the blessings of Christianity—in proportion as our religion is personal shall we be interested in the welfare of others. Oh, that our love might grow deeper and broader—more real and more universal! How happy should we be with larger and more Christ-like interests—blest ourselves, indeed, while seeking under God to bless others!—*O Lord, expand and strengthen my sympathies, and grant that I may witness to Thy love.*

September 20th.

Christ Jesus has gone before us in life and in death. He has gone before us to lead us into fuller life. He died—His spirit was separated from His body—while His spirit was in Paradise, His body lay in the grave; He rose—He lived again in the body; He lives in Heaven. He is our Forerunner and our Helper—let us follow and be helped by Him.—*Lord Jesus, bid me look to Thee.*

September 21st. (S. Matthew.)

It is the heart for which God asks, and, moreover, it is the *whole* heart. There are many claimants in the world for our heart's affections; but, in withholding our hearts from these and giving them to God, we give Him our best—we give Him our all—we give Him ourselves. Oh, that we might lose ourselves in loving, thorough-going service, and self-dedication!—*O God, save me from half-heartedness—grant that my heart may be whole with Thee.*

September 22nd.

After this life there is a future, call it existence or call it life—it will last for ever. The character of this future state will depend upon our use or abuse of this present world—our life here—our day of salvation. Are we living for the future—attending to present duty—watching as well as praying—practising as well as professing?—*Teach me, Lord, so to live, that, when I come to die, I may be nearer to Thee.*

September 23rd.

In the journey of life we must take care not to be puffed up with an idea of our own importance, but to have due consideration for others. We must, as Christians, have the spiritual welfare of our brethren at heart—we must not, by any waywardness or wilfulness of our own, put any stumbling block in their way—on the contrary, we must be influenced by kindly regard to them.—*Lord Jesus, make me humble, gentle, and forbearing.*

September 24th.

Our cornfields point us to the unchanging God, Who, true to His promise, has ever kept His great world-covenant. It is necessary that we should be given now to prayer, and now to thanksgiving, in order that there may be kept alive within us a sense of our dependence upon God. We must not forget the great and merciful God Who delights to visit us in mercy and loving-kindness.—*Make me, O God, trustful, dutiful, and thankful.*

September 25th.

When we learn to view everything in the light of eternity, we then see that it is our wisdom to cast away all occasions of sin—all that may lead us to sin, to cut off or pluck out anything which may hinder the main work of our salvation—endanger our eternal welfare. How real the future becomes to the believer—how solemn does life appear!—*Give me a right judgment, O Lord, and make me wisehearted.*

September 26th.

As inhabitants of a fallen world where persons of different dispositions—different temperaments—different prejudices have to live together, though it is not for us to give up all right to our opinions, it is for us, without foolish cavilling, and party spirit, to be ready to seek the *real* profit of others —not to hinder, but to help—not to endanger, but to save. —*Grant, O God, that, in my dealings with others, I may be more like Christ.*

September 27th.

We must try to be cheerful in our daily life. Our present efforts after good must not be weakened by vain regrets over past follies—we want all the energy and courage we can get to attack our present duty—we must not allow any depression of spirit to hinder us. Remorse will lead to despair, but repentance must lead us to increased loving effort.—*Teach me, O God, to " act in the living present."*

September 28th.

Days such as those appointed as Harvest Festivals help to fix great truths in our minds; it is well that again and again we should be reminded, that, behind and above what we call the laws of nature, God *is*, and that He is continually *working* for our good—that we are dependent upon Him—that we have Him to ask, and Him to thank for all.—*Make me, O God, habitually prayerful and thankful.*

September 29th. (S. Michael and All Angels.)

Do we not believe in the holy Angels? The Bible tells us of their worship of God in Heaven—of their good offices to the faithful on earth. How much we lose by failing to grasp what is revealed to us of them! Engaged in our daily work—taking our nightly rest—on our knees in earnest devotion, they are by our side.—*Lord, that I may worship Thee, serve Thee, and obey Thee as I ought to do!*

September 30th.

We come—we go—we work—we cease from work—we live—we die; but, in God's good time, after all the scatterings and separations of earth, in life and in death, there will come the great ingathering; and the faithful of every age, country, and tongue, shall be "clothed upon with their house which is from Heaven" to be with Christ in glory.—*Grant, Lord, that, at the harvest of souls, I may be found amongst the good wheat.*

October 1st.

As obedience leads to happiness, so disobedience to unhappiness—this is a very true way of looking at things. God has left much in our own power, and we may make ourselves very wretched—the very misery which God has attached to a course of wrong-doing should deter men from it. It is a proof that right is right, that the pursuit of it has a tendency to make people so cheerful and happy.—*Make me ready and happy, O God, to do Thy will.*

October 2nd.

How much is often contained in one little verse!—"trust in the Lord and be doing good." God is one to be trusted—we must be trusting. God has done *that* for us which calls for our love—we must be up and doing as servants of God. Consider, then, what God is, and what we ought to be—what God has done, and what we ought to do.—*Grant that I may trust in Thee, O God, and try to do my best.*

October 3rd.

The intercession of Christ for us in Heaven is a great reality—He is the High Priest of His people. Scripture does not tell us how it is carried on—all is wrapped to the last in figure—He is the Lamb slain. Merit is His, and our poor offerings, having no merit of their own, He takes and presents, and they are accepted for His sake.—*Make me, O Father, to love that phrase "through Jesus Christ our Lord."*

October 4th.

We all have our ups and downs in life—the path of life is varied—the time is short, and death will come. The true way of testing the nature and character both of our joys and sorrows is to ask, will they last?—there are no real evils, and no real joys, but those that are lasting — *Teach us to number our days, O God, that we may apply our hearts unto wisdom.*

October 5th.

As Christians we ought to resign all self-interest which is irreconcileable with our *true* self-interest—to deny ourselves, as followers of Jesus Christ, in all those things which hinder our hopes for the life eternal. Self-denial was a prominent feature of our Redeemer's character, and played an important part in His life on earth. Are our lives in harmony with Christ's life?—*Give me, Lord Jesus, a right understanding of the Christian life.*

October 6th.

What is our love towards God? Do we ever put anything in the place of God—any gift which He has given us? Do we put any object of affection in the place of the Maker and Giver of all? Do we love ourselves—our own wills—our own schemes—purposes—pleasures—ease better than we love God? Do we set up any idol in our hearts?—*O God, make me to love Thee above all.*

October 7th.

We lose much by want of definiteness in our religious life. We talk about penitence—faith—thankfulness, and so forth; but what have we to shew of these? Can we point to any act of penitence—any act of faith—any act of thankfulness? Can we point to any definite thing in which we have shewn our penitence—our faith—our thankfulness, as a proof that we know what we talk about?—*Grant me, Lord, consistency of life.*

October 8th.

We do not know how long we have to live here. We must try to use life aright—to persevere in well-doing—to be given to cheerful activity—to go forward in hopefulness of spirit, taking the Scriptures for our guide, and seeking grace through Holy Communion and prayer. Oh, that God's will may be done in us and by us!—*Lord God, let Thy presence go with me.*

October 9th.

Is it not to be feared that many are frittering away the time which they should be spending in seeking their own true good, and in doing what good they can in the world around them, in finding fault with others? This is very poor sort of work—it eats away our strength and energy, acting very detrimentally upon ourselves.—*Save me, good Lord, from this evil spirit, and create a better mind within me.*

October 10th.

Are we getting good habits? Habits can only be acquired by repeated action. By accustoming ourselves to act in the same manner again and again, we get into a habit. It is a good thing, when called upon to act, to find it more or less natural to us, having formed a good habit, to do the right thing.—*Lord, grant that I may so live, that I may delight in what is right.*

October 11th.

Are we attending to our various duties—duties which come before us every day, and demand our attention? We must remember that all the different relationships of life, in which we find ourselves, involve duties—we cannot innocently escape from them—we cannot avoid them without incurring guilt; they are ours—they wait to be fulfilled. Do we recognize our duties, and try to do them well?—*Give me grace, Lord, to adorn the different relationships of life.*

October 12th.

Remember that you are strangers and pilgrims here, and try to live in character with your name—often thinking of your true citizenship—making that use of this world which is according to the will of God—having well-regulated affections—going forward contentedly and happily. Oh, that our pilgrimage may have a happy end—that we may find Heaven to be a happy home!—*Guide me continually, O Lord, and, after this life, receive me into Thy glory.*

October 13th.

How difficult constantly to realize God's presence! Clouds obscure the light—our sins separate us from God—yea, our little faults hide His face from us—" the pure in heart shall see God "—alas, how much we may interpose between ourselves and the Sun of Righteousness! We ought to walk as children of light and of the day (not afraid of the light)—we ought, as Christians, to be light-bearers in the world.—*Lord, that I may walk in the light of Thy truth!*

October 14th.

As the practice of godliness is not to be acquired in a day, even so vice is not to be subdued in a day—our adversary cannot be knocked down at one blow. Truly, the Christian's is a work of *crucifying* the old man, for he dies lingeringly—experience bears all this out, and shews us that it is no easy thing to lead a Christian life.—*Lord, grant me Christian endurance, and Christian victory.*

October 15th.

God knows our hearts, and whether they are inclined to keep His laws. Are we living in the daily pursuit of righteousness—desiring to do the thing that is right? For the most part we know our duty—we shall not perish for lack of knowledge; but what is knowledge without love? it leaves the affections untouched—it will never warm us up to duty, nor spur us on to obedience.—*Give me, Lord, a good understanding, and a loving heart.*

October 16th.

When God bids us do anything, He is always ready to help us to do it—He knows that we need His help, and He is willing to give it. He calls upon us to do what we cannot do without His help, because He would have us put forth those efforts of our own, which He requires to see made by those on whom He would bestow His grace.—*Lord, speak but the word, and I will quietly do my best.*

October 17th.

It is most desirable and important to lay stress on the great facts of historical Christianity, because there is a spirit of infidelity abroad which disputes these facts, and also because there is a great deal of sickly sentiment, which, reducing religion to a mere matter of feeling, neglects the grand objective truths, standing forth as quite distinct from ourselves, which lie at the foundation of our religion.—*O God, confirm me in the Faith.*

October 18th. (S. Luke.)

Christ is our kind Physician—the work of Christianity is a work of healing. It is most important that we should bear this in mind—it is not mere development that we want, but we stand in need of healing—we require not mere food, but medicine. We must take no false views of the Gospel. Christianity gives us just what we want—a remedy for the sin which God hates.—*Lord Jesus, I am sick, pity me.*

October 19th.

Half-hearted people only half believe; the hearty Christian, the whole-hearted Christian, is one who is persuaded—convinced—has a grasp of the truth, and his faith blossoms and brings forth fruit. Grasp the truth, and you cannot live a lie; live a lie, and you cannot say that you have grasped the truth. Let us mark well, then, how practical our religion is!—*Grant, O God, that I may be whole-hearted, and thoroughly devoted to Thee.*

October 20th.

We should be continually striving after progress, only looking to the past more truly to repent of its sins—to be filled with thankfulness for its mercies—to gather experience for the future—rising higher and higher to a newer and newer life—every day beginning afresh with earnest prayer to God—making continual vigorous starts. Every time we come to Holy Communion we make newness of life a subject of prayer.—*Renew, O God, my will from day to day.*

October 21st.

We have entered into covenant with God—our Christian name reminds us of the covenant. It is not enough that Christ our Passover has been sacrificed for us, we want to be sprinkled, as by faith we may be sprinkled, with the atoning blood—we want our religion to be a personal and individual thing. I want to know that what Christ has done for *all* men, He has done for *me*.—*Make me thankful, Lord, for the Sacraments of the Gospel.*

October 22nd.

Whatever our position in life, the same reward is set before us by the same loving Father—we have to look forward to the same eternal prospects—we are all fellow-travellers to the heavenly city; whether we fill a high or a low place *now*, it matters not so long as we live and act faithfully—seeking to fill that place well, and to do our duty well.—*Lord, grant that my life may be full of hope and duty.*

October 23rd.

Is the service which we give to God a loving service? Whether it be the service which we offer to God in His House, or that service which we render to God in the world—the service of worship, or the service of work, love ought to be the motive power urging us on—love ought to impart character to it.—*Pour love into my heart, O God, that I may shew forth Thy praise, not only with my lips, but in my life.*

October 24th.

Delay in spiritual things is always dangerous; not only on account of the uncertainty of life, but also because every day enlarges our task, while it lessens our capabilities of performing it—the enemy grows stronger, and we grow weaker—our energy grows less, and we become more and more the servants of our besetting sin. Arise then at once!
—*Teach me, O God, the worth of the present, and make me alive to duty.*

October 25th.

The Being of God is mysterious, and so are His ways—His ways are in the sea—His path in the great waters—His footsteps are not known—clouds and darkness are round about Him—He dwells in the unapproachable light. But, is there not a most true knowledge of God that is learnt upon the knees?—we thus *feel* Him out, and gain that knowledge which comes from love.—*O my God, be ever near me.*

October 26th.

When we find men hating the evil which they once loved—making a real sacrifice for the sake of truth and duty—keeping out of the way of temptation—doing what they can to screen or to rescue others from danger, earnestly seeking their good; depend upon it, you see signs of the Holy Spirit's working in their hearts and lives—God is truly with them!—*Grant, Lord, that I may know Thy Spirit's power.*

~~~~~~~~~~~~

October 27th.

Satan is very subtle. If we are trying to serve God, he may not tempt us to open rebellion against Him, he may allow us to say our prayers—to read our Bible—to go to Church—yes, even to the Lord's Holy Table, but he will do his best to rob our prayers of fervour—to make Bible truth ineffective—to make our Church-going and Communions formal.—*Good Lord, deliver me from Satan's devices.*

~~~~~~~~~~~~

October 28th. (SS. Simon and Jude.)

We are differently constituted, and have our different characteristic features, but we must all seek to be good Christians. What help we may find in studying the lives of God's Saints in the Bible! We may learn from the examples, there displayed to view, what to acquire—what to avoid—what to seek after—what to shun, in order that our lives may be just towards men, and pleasing to God.—*Make me to follow, Lord, in the way of Thy holy ones.*

~~~~~~~~~~~~

October 29th.

Life has its duties, belonging to its several stages—childhood—youth—maturity. Doors are continually being opened, yes, and shut behind us—are we doing our best to avail ourselves of all our opportunities?—how sad to feel that any should have come and gone unused—there is no bringing them back! What of the penalty now—hereafter?—better to suffer now, if our suffering only lead us to repent.—*Lord, make me alive to my duty.*

October 30th.

He Who was made flesh and dwelt among us—the anointed of God—the Lord Jesus Christ, when on earth, concerned Himself about men's bodies, as well as their souls—He Who came to save the soul is also the Saviour of the body. We must not despise the body—we must take care of it—keep it as the Temple of the Holy Ghost—bought with a price, we must glorify God in our bodies.—*Lord God, sanctify me wholly.*

October 31st.

Take God at His word—make a holy venture, and you shall find to your delight how true and faithful He is—"taste and see how gracious the Lord is." Exercise your faith, and then will come the *blessedness* of believing—great will be the influence upon our lives; and the faith, which now urges us on to loving work, will one day be lost in sight.—*Lord, give me faith and happiness in Thee.*

November 1st. (All Saints' Day.)

May we not think of those who have fallen asleep in Jesus as witnessing us, looking upon us, seeing all that we do—the race we are running—the battle we are fighting—the journey we are making? May we not think of them also as having witnessed *for* us?—their examples speak to us—their lives tell us how good it is to live near to God.—*Make me, good Lord, a witness for Thee.*

November 2nd.

Is not the assembling of ourselves together a good and pleasant thing? Christian people are thus knit in one, and are led to feel how many things they have in common—how similar are their wants—how similar the consolation needed; happy, indeed, if led to feel of one heart and soul, united in one holy bond of truth—peace—faith—charity.—*Lord Jesus, draw us together by drawing us to Thyself.*

November 3rd.

Do we cherish wrong desires—allow ourselves in some sinful passion—go on still in wickedness, and expect to be delivered from the wrath to come—to be saved from ourselves, as it were, by a miracle? The good, just, and merciful God will save us only in His own way—it is not for us to dictate terms of our own.—*Grant, Lord, that I may shew forth in my life the obedience of faith.*

November 4th.

As often as I find it difficult to fight against sin and Satan, I can with truth say I am not alone in the battle—I have many fellow-soldiers, and my lot is no harder than theirs! May we not encourage one another?—May we not be encouraged by one another? We are fighting under the same banner—the same Captain; and God is with us.—*Lord, bid me be of good courage.*

November 5th.

Thoughtful sometimes it may be, how many are thoughtless much more frequently than they are thoughtful. It is the duty of the Christian to watch, but a thoughtless person does *not* watch. We need to be more thoughtful and self-collected, as we go on from day to day; we need a steady habit of thoughtfulness—an undercurrent of quiet thought, so that nothing shall surprise us or worst us, when off our guard.—*Lord, save me from distraction.*

November 6th.

We must always take care rightly to divide the Word of Truth—to compare Scripture with Scripture, so as to see the whole truth in its due proportions. The promise must not be taken without its condition—the word of comfort without the word of warning—the statement without the counter-statement. Half-truths are very dangerous—how many have gone astray by neglecting to read the Bible carefully!—*Help me, O God, in the study of Thy Word.*

November 7th.

How lightly do men generally think of sins of omission—far otherwise does God view them! Our Church teaches us to confess them amongst, if not before, others—how often, too, does Holy Scripture impress upon us their condemnatory character. We must repent of our neglect. Look the matter straight in the face—how much—how many duties have we left undone!—*Pardon, Lord, my neglect of duty, my neglect of Thee and Thine.*

November 8th.

It may be, looking back on the past, we can remember a time when our love was warmer than it is now. Why have we left our first love? Why have we allowed our love to cool? Why are we not so earnest in work, and fervent in devotion, as we once were? Have the lukewarm ones of the world reduced us to what we are?—*Stir up, O Lord, my will and affections.*

November 9th.

What a thought is the thought of God, it lifts us above the world—absorbs all other thoughts—occupies the whole mind! When we give ourselves up to think of God, we become lost in wonder, love and praise. The thought of God is a satisfying thought—a happy thought. Thrice happy shall we be, if we can individually claim an interest in God—believing in His individualizing love and care.—*O God, grant that I may find happiness in the thought of Thee.*

November 10th.

If we would grow strong in the spiritual life, it is necessary that we should know our natural weakness—there is a tendency in man to over-rate his own strength. We are weak in ourselves, and only strong in our dependence upon God—" when I am weak, then am I strong." We ought to live in a spirit of continued and sustained dependence.—*Lord, draw me to the Throne of Grace, that, through prayers and Sacraments faithfully used, strength may be ministered to me.*

November 11th.

We must not allow ourselves to speak in that one-sided way, so common, of the visitations of God, as if God only visited the world in the time of earthquake—war—famine—pestilence—sickness—sudden death — great calamities. God visits us every day in mercy and loving-kindness — not to kill but to keep alive. He gives us food—happiness—comfort—every true blessing. He deals with us as the great Father of all.—*Be ever with me, O God, for, without Thee, I cannot live.*

November 12th.

Are we always honest with ourselves? Do we not sometimes try to please ourselves without displeasing God? —this means trying to reconcile evil with good—wickedness with duty. We cannot change the will of God—we may however deceive and blind ourselves. First thoughts are often the best, at any rate in matters of duty.—*Give me, Lord, peace of mind, and a simple desire to obey Thee at any cost.*

November 13th.

I stand beside the Holy One and feel my own sinfulness—I stand beside the Obedient One and mark how, in His life, the Father was glorified—I stand beside the Perfect One and feel how poor are my efforts—I stand beside the Crucified One and learn that God is not only light, but also love; I take courage, trusting in His merits, relying on His help—I make an attempt (poor as the result may be) to follow His example.—*Grant me, Lord, to be faithful to the end.*

November 14th.

Christianity teaches us to pray for others, and to exert ourselves for the good of others. Oh, that whenever we pray for ourselves, we might pray for others also, as if their needs were our own, and that our work might have no selfishness about it! In proportion to the reality of our own spiritual life will be our real interest in the welfare of others.—*Lord, bind us together, not as tares, but as good wheat.*

November 15th.

Am I a creature of time, or a pilgrim passing onward to the eternal city? Do I accustom myself to look forward, till eternity becomes quite real to me, and Heaven like my home? Let us seek to have such a realizing grasp of the things unseen, that our whole life may be influenced for good—that we may live for the great Future.—*Grant me, O God, so to pass through things temporal that I finally lose not the things eternal.*

November 16th.

Looking in faith to Jesus the Crucified, we cannot fail to become personally enriched—good will come to us—strength will be ministered to us to go on in the path of holiness, to become more complete, more perfect in obedience, more entire and thorough in the surrender of ourselves to the will of God.—*O Father, make me to know the unsearchable riches of Christ.*

November 17th.

What is our religious state? Is there any deadness about us in any part? Does a deadness ever creep over us, or do we feel that we are becoming more and more alive? Christ is the Quickener of souls—the Food of the divine life in us. Oh, that we may live through Him—live, and not have a mere name to live!—*O Christ, hear me—save me from death—give me fuller life.*

November 18th.

Happy is the knowledge which comes from obedience! Doing the will of God, we shall learn to know Him better; there is much to be gained by cheerful obedience, obedience will increase our knowledge and love of the truth. Do evil, and you will love the darkness rather than light, and the truth will be hidden from your view—act rightly, and you will see the truth more clearly, and love it well.—*O Lord God, reveal Thyself and Thy truth to me more fully.*

November 19th.

What should we say of Englishmen travelling in a foreign country, if they were to forget the habits and proprieties of home—the observance of the Lord's Day—the different restraints which we are accustomed to put upon ourselves, and accommodated themselves to the customs and practices of the country in which they were, for the time being, sojourning? God is everywhere. We must live consistent lives.—*Teach me, O Father, wherever I may be, to live always as Thy child.*

November 20th.

A life of trust, and a life of loving service are but two phases of one and the same life—faith and obedience are separate in idea, but in the life they are one. In thinking of God's grace, we must not forget our duty. Oh, for more of the active spirit of Christianity! Oh, for more Christian living! We want to see people acting on high Christian principles, shewing the love, constancy, and perseverance of Christian believers.—*Lord, grant me both the body and the spirit of Christianity.*

November 21st.

Belief in the future life of glory invigorates me. Strength comes to me—the power of Christ's resurrection, and I am urged on in the path of duty. Life here, with all its doings, fightings, and sufferings, I can bear. The resurrection of Christ the First-fruits and the Forerunner, which puts the seal to all other Christian truth, believed in, nerves me to do, and brave, and suffer all—it spurs me on to live the Christian life.—*Give me, Lord, persuasion of Thy truth.*

November 22nd.

Just as in the world of nature God fits everything for its position, so God orders the different lots of men, and offers them needful help. None of us should complain, because we think ourselves placed at a disadvantage; for, God knowing all, is ready with divine aid. We must not look to success in the spiritual life as depending upon circumstances, but upon the grace of God received, and faithfully used.—*Grant, O my God, that I may live and serve Thee as I ought.*

November 23rd.

The Christian is called to walk in newness of life, as one who is alive, as one who is holy, as one who is free—to walk with God—to walk in love—to walk in the Spirit. Are we walking thus—are we resolved so to do—what has been our success in the past—what of the future? Does the past give us hope for the future?—*Help me, Lord, to be true to my Christian calling.*

November 24th.

Some there are who *reject* divine truth—how many more there are who *neglect* it; these last do not go so far as the former—they live in simple neglect of truth and duty—divine things are matters of indifference to them—let them know that neglect is enough to bring them to ruin. Do we ever find this spirit of neglect and indifference stealing over ourselves in any way? - *Good Lord, grant that this spirit be not mine.*

November 25th.

How shall God guide us, if, when He looks down upon us, He does not find us looking up to Him—if He finds that our attention is arrested in another direction? Let us look up to God in faith—faith is the spiritual sense of sight. God looks upon us to lead us onward—let us walk by faith, and He shall guide our feet into the way of peace. —*Make me willing, Lord, to be guided by Thee.*

November 26th.

We are plainly taught in the Bible, and experience confirms the teaching, that we cannot be happy unless we are seeking to be good—that obedience is the condition of happiness—that happiness is to be sought in trying to please God; no other way can be devised—we may defy the whole world to find out any other way to happiness—it is the road the Saviour trod.—*Lord Jesus, I would follow Thee, assist me by Thy grace.*

November 27th.

Let us think as we ought of God's individual providence over our own lives. Let us think of the Father's care for each of His children—how He watches over each individually. Looking to the *past*, we may see how it has been with us—we feel His hand upon us *now*, and, as to the *future*, we can trust Him. To God each of us can pray as if His ear were attentive to him alone.—*Hitherto Thou hast helped me, O God, help me still.*

November 28th.

If we pray for our clergy, we partake in their work, we are with them, so to speak, in their studies—in their preparation for the pulpit—in their visitation—in all their parish work. We strengthen their hands by our prayers, and help to make their ministrations powerful; we bless them in their lives, and support them in their labours by our prayers.—*Lord, grant that I may think of this, and never neglect this duty.*

November 29th.

It is now the fashion to set apart certain days for the concentration of our thoughts on different Christian works which need our support—not only have we a day of intercession for Foreign Missions, but our attention is also directed to various operations of the Church at home, and, in many places, there is the Hospital Sunday—all this is well. We are reminded at definite times of duties and privileges which ought never to be forgotten.—*Good Lord, warm this heart of mine.*

November 30th. (S. Andrew.)

S. Andrew shews a true missionary spirit—he no sooner finds Christ for himself, than he goes to find his brother, and brings him to Jesus. This was a good beginning as a missionary. So ought it to be with us all—charity should begin at home, and go forth thence to warm the world. Our interest ought first to be shewn within the narrow circle, and then to grow larger and wider, until it embraces all for whom Christ died.—*Grant, Lord, that my love may thus grow.*

December 1st.

Well may this present life be called night—the visible presence of Christ is withdrawn from us—we are awaiting the return of the Sun of Righteousness; all slumber and sleep—the darkness of ignorance is around—there is many a path of danger into which we may stray—the night seems sometimes very gloomy—there is no brightness in it; we would gladly welcome the bright light of day.—*Lighten mine eyes that I sleep not in death.*

December 2nd.

This present life is sometimes spoken of as the night—sometimes as the day, and so in a very true sense it is—the day of work, opportunities, and hopes. Very truly may we speak of the daytime of life—the night *cometh.* What, then, do we look for as Christians?—rest, indeed, and yet a night that shall be as day—a brighter and more cloudless day, not a darker and more dismal night.—*O Day Star, arise in my heart!*

December 3rd.

What is it to be asleep—to be a sleeper? When we are asleep realities are nothing to us, while unrealities are everything. What is it to awake out of sleep? The result of awaking is this, that things seem and appear what they really are—not as they so often seem and appear to us. Are we asleep or awake?—perhaps not wide awake—dreaming, though sometimes disturbed in our dreams.—*Lord, make me mindful of the last great trumpet-blowing.*

December 4th.

We are taught to pray for the appearing of Christ's Kingdom. May we not do so heartily, sinful though we be, provided we are with earnestness and diligence striving to live soberly, righteously, and godly in this present world, intent on pleasing God, and thinking not only of our salvation, but of His glory? There need be, in such case, no shrinking from the Judge.—*Grant, O Lord, that I may dread nothing but sin.*

December 5th.

Deal kindly with those who differ from yourself—avoid proud looks—abstain from hard words—speak gently—bear and forbear. Do not think too highly of yourself, nor be too ready to take offence. Be courteous and generous in your conduct, humble and obliging.—*Jesus, Master, teach me to move about amongst my fellows, mindful that we shall all have to stand together before Thy Judgment Throne.*

December 6th.

Let us who still live here on earth take example from those who have gone before us—let us treasure the memory of those who have lived for God—who have led eminently Christian lives in the world. The examples of such may be of immense service to us—may we follow them as they have followed Christ, hoping, in the great Resurrection-day, to be together in Heaven's happy company!—*Lord, grant that I may be an imitator of those who inherit the promises.*

December 7th.

While time is ours, let us listen to God's voice, come to us as it may—while the day of opportunity lingers, let us " work out our own salvation with fear and trembling "—while there is hope, let us not despair—while the Saviour waits to heal, let us seek His saving grace; so that when the battle is over—the course finished—the journey ended, all may be well.—*Lord Jesus, prepare me for Thy coming.*

December 8th.

We must remember that, whatever our position in life, we are all candidates for the same Heavenly reward—all servants of Jesus Christ, and shall all stand together to be judged. Shall we not, then, put a check upon all unkind words, all ungenerous thoughts—shall we not try to shew gentle consideration to all, and to help one another in a loving spirit?—*Press home to me, O God, some of those passages of Thy Word which tell us of mutual Christian duties.*

December 9th.

That our Lord after He rose, shewing that He had atoned for our sins—that His sacrifice had been accepted, ascended into Heaven in our nature is a fact of great comfort—we have one belonging to us in Heaven. That our Lord ascended while blessing those whom He was leaving is, too, a great consolation. He will come again in like manner—oh, that He may have a blessing for me!—*Teach me, Lord Jesus, to look for Thine appearing.*

December 10th.

All God's dealings with us are designed for our profit—for our good, yes, even the sharp pruning knife—the corrections which cause us to smart; but God deals with us also in that prosperity in which we so often fail to recognise His hand. What fruit are we bearing? Remember the fig-tree in the vineyard, if it bear fruit—if not.—*Grant, Lord, that I may be rightly exercised by Thy dealings with me.*

December 11th.

Do we look for His appearing Who died for us? Shall we love His appearing Who rose and ascended into Heaven for us? Are we in very truth getting ready to meet Him Who went before to prepare a place for His faithful people? Are we given to any evil practices which His Word condemns, so that we fear His coming? Do we love the world of sense more than His spiritual Kingdom?—*Make me fit for a place, Lord, in Thy new creation.*

December 12th.

The truth of the resurrection of the dead rests on historical facts—our resurrection is bound up with Christ's resurrection. We are being continually reminded, in this world, that we have to die; but the human heart craves for immortality—for a higher life—a life above and beyond the present. To such a life we are called, and for it we are exhorted to prepare.—*Lord Jesus, Thou hast gone on before, bid me look to Thee.*

December 13th.

Love planned our redemption—love was the moving cause of all that wonderful transaction on our behalf. Our Christian service will never be anything of what it ought to be, unless we love our Saviour, and are ready to forgive as God is ready to forgive us. We may find it hard to tread along the narrow way, but the complexion of all will be changed if we love Christ— if we know that we are walking along the road in which the Lord Jesus Whom we love is to be found.—*Give me, Lord, a sense of Thy love to me.*

December 14th.

Two things incapacitate us from judging our brethren rightly—the one is the absence of trial, and the other the presence of sin. Those who have never been tried often form harsh judgments, while those who are frequently falling become weak and inconsistent. Jesus Christ was tempted, but did not yield to sin. His sympathy is perfect—His mind is correct. Every condition is fulfilled in Him to render Him a most just Judge.—*Good Lord, prepare me for the Judgment.*

December 15th.

We know not how long or how short the time may be, but " we look for the resurrection of the dead, and the life of the world to come." We shall all be summoned before the Judgment Seat of Christ. With what feelings do we look forward to resurrection and judgment ? Are we using this world as the gate of Heaven? Have we already risen in heart and mind?—*Grant me, Lord, the daily renewing of Thy Holy Spirit.*

December 16th.

Can you say—Religion has become to me an all-absorbing matter—I live amongst realities—by faith I walk each day—in the surely-grounded hope of a happy Hereafter, I press forward—I trace every blessing to a Father's love—for the forgiveness of my sins, I plead the sacrifice once offered—for strength to fight my life-long battle, I seek the Spirit's aid—I have learnt to look above in work and prayer, to look to the end?—*Grant, O Lord, that I may be full of faith, and hope, and love.*

December 17th.

Are we living so that God's blessing may come upon us? Are we walking in the light as He is in the light—walking from day to day in the path of life, on which falls the shadow of the Cross of Him Whose blood cleanseth from sin? If we would have the blessing, we must be among the waiting—the expectant ones patiently looking upwards in faith.—*Guide me in Thy ways, O God, and bless me.*

December 18th.

Are we wanting in that ready endurance of hardness which is a qualification for good service in the Christian army? Let us be warmed by the example of those who have fought in the world for Christ—whose lives speak to us of love and self-sacrifice. Let us be minded to make this Advent Season a new starting point for increased discipline and holy effort.—*O Lord, bid me be of good courage—brave in suffering and in action.*

December 19th.

It is wise and good for us to look realities in the face. The sins of the past may be blotted out by the blood of Christ—but what of the present and the future? What are we aiming at in life—what are our thoughts and desires—what have we in view? Are we ready for Christ's appearing—do we look for Him—is the thought of His Second Coming a glad thought?—*Good Lord, prepare me for Thy Advent.*

December 20th.

If we are really in earnest, and desirous of doing what is right, God will help us by His grace. Remember the answer of childhood—" Yes, verily, and by God's help so I will." Without the assurance of divine assistance it would be vain and foolish to make any resolve or promise, but with that assurance none who are sincere and truthful need be afraid.—*Lord, bid me go forth in Thy strength, and grant me true success.*

December 21st. (S. Thomas.)

Some find it far easier to believe than others. To-day we think of S. Thomas, to whom the Lord Jesus said "become not faithless, but believing." He was doubting our Lord's Resurrection—hovering between faith and unbelief; he felt that great issues were at stake—he would not lightly be convinced. When he did believe, however, he believed with all his heart. How is it with me?—*Make me, O God, to adore the Mystery of the Holy Incarnation, and make my religion as real as Thy Son's Resurrection.*

December 22nd.

Are we to mourn for our friends who have died in Christ as separated from us? We may wonder how the *heathen* could bear the pain of parting with those dear to them. It is for *us*, however, to know that we are all members of one great family? Is there not to be a glorious re-union in the presence of God—union in Paradise—union in Heaven; shall not that modify our grief?—*Be Thou my Comforter, O God.*

December 23rd.

There is a Kingdom which cannot be moved. However unsettled, tottering, and changeful, things around us may seem, God is above all, ruling according to His wise providence—the King of a mighty and enduring Kingdom. It is not for us to be too firmly rooted here. Have faith in God!—let us not fear nor be dismayed. Oh, that we may stand in our lot at the end of the days!—*Grant me grace, O God, to persevere.*

December 24th.

We must try to profit by that power which comes to us throught the incarnation of our Blessed Saviour, that we may grow more and more into His likeness, and be what true sons ought to be. The Son of God became the Son of Man that we might be adopted by the Heavenly Father as sons. Jesus as God will enable us to follow the example which He set us as man.—*Make me, dear Lord, a new creature.*

December 25th. (Christmas Day.)

When we think of the birth of Jesus Christ as the promised One Who came to satisfy the wants of fallen man—when we think of the birth of Jesus Christ as the manifestation of God's grace, and the opening up of a channel of grace as well as the pledge of future blessings, shall we not pray that He may be born in us that *now* we may live, and *hereafter* rise together with Him?—*Lord Jesus, come to me.*

December 26th. (S. Stephen.)

S. Stephen was sustained and strengthened in the hour of death by a most glorious vision—he saw, in the opened Heavens, Jesus as the Son of Man standing as it were ready to defend him, and receive him. He who saw this vision was full of the Holy Ghost—that same blessed Spirit will bring Christ near to us, and be our Comforter in life, and in death.—*O Holy Dove, fly not away—never leave me.*

December 27th. (S. John.)

Light is composed of different coloured rays which are differently absorbed by the various objects on which they fall—hence the colour which they assume. As in the natural, so in the spiritual—God is Light. S. John is noted for his *love*, there was that in him which made a special response to the love of God in Christ. Love made him quick-sighted, and led to a lifelong consecration of his being to the service of his Master.—*Let Thy light, O Lord, shine upon me.*

December 28th. (Holy Innocents.)

Our Church, following in the steps of Holy Scripture, bids us, at least one day in the year, contemplate the state of childhood. We cannot remain children—we cannot keep the purity which consists in the ignorance of evil, but we may, repenting and believing, yield to our God a hearty obedience, and willingly choose to take upon ourselves His holy service.—*Grant, Lord, that, in all right ways, I may never cease to be childlike.*

December 29th.

God's forbearance is only dimly shadowed forth by that of the tenderest earthly parent—the human fails to shew forth the divine. How is it that God bears so long and patiently with us? Is not the love of our Father, which prompted Him to send His only-begotten Son as a little child into a fallen world, a full explanation of all the wonderful goodness which we have experienced?—*Grant, Lord, that I may shew forth my thankfulness by striving to imitate Thee.*

December 30th.

Time past, it is true, cannot be recalled, but we should endeavour, as far as possible, to recover what we have lost by a double diligence in improving the time that remains. Let us so order our actions that we may live much in little space. Let us consider time as a sacred trust from God, and strive to spend each day holier than the previous one.—*Grant, Lord, that I may take to heart the Apostle's words " redeeming the time."*

December 31st.

Have we made any real progress in the spiritual life during the past year—after so many Sundays—so many means of improvement afforded us? Have we been trying to do our duty more thoroughly—to live more continuously in God's realized presence—to walk more constantly in the light? How far have we succeeded in living a life pleasing to God—the life of faithful progress?—*Help me, O God, to make, and carry out all good resolutions.*

Appendix.

Ash Wednesday.

It is well that we should have a considerable portion of the Church's year set apart for special recollectedness, reflection, and devotional exercises—for taking measure of ourselves, comparing ourselves with the divine rule—for coming before God as sinners—for laying hold on Him in Whom was no sin (made sin for us), seeking ever to deepen our repentance—seeking help to overcome—seeking eternal salvation.—*Grant, Lord, that I may use all opportunities for good.*

Good Friday.

We must learn beneath the Cross of Christ—we must look to the Saviour and mark His dying love—we must linger around the death-scene of the Son of God until our hearts receive the impression of the Cross upon them. Then, wherever our lot may be cast—whatever our work may be, we must daily seek the blood that washes white—the blood of sprinkling.—*Make me, Lord God, to walk in Thy truth.*

Easter Day.

Let each Easter Day mark a period in our lives—make a point in life's journey. Truly it is a joyful day on which we commemorate the triumph of the Victor—the Resurrection of Jesus Christ. In Him we have hope for ourselves, and for others. Hoping for the resurrection-life we will live for it—the love of Heaven shall kill all sinful affections of earth.—*Grant, Lord, that I may have part in the resurrection of the just.*

Ascension Day.

It was to man's advantage that our Lord ascended into Heaven, that His influence might not be limited to the few, but vouchsafed to the many—that far and wide the influence of the Saviour might be felt. Had He remained on earth, the number of those who could have enjoyed His presence at any one time must have been limited—He was exalted that He might be the joy of the whole earth.—*Jesus, King of Glory, do Thou rule in my heart.*

Whit Sunday.

The Holy Spirit is so called because, of the Three Persons of the Blessed Trinity, it is His particular office to speak to the spirit within us, and to make us holy. He came to finish *in us* what Christ had finished *in Himself*, to form in us a Christ-like character—to make us like Christ, working in us—making us holy—carrying on Christ's work in our hearts.—*Dwell in my heart, O God, and rule in my life.*

Trinity Sunday.

The doctrine of the Trinity in Unity is a most important doctrine—of great practical importance. It is interwoven with Christianity—it winds itself round the whole scheme of our redemption—no less than our salvation is involved in it—with it Christianity stands or falls. That it has its bearing upon our everyday practice—everyday life is plainly to be seen.—*Make me, Lord, so to love Thee, that I may ever be ready to contend earnestly for Thy truth.*

www.ingramcontent.com/pod-product-compliance
Lightning Source LLC
Chambersburg PA
CBHW020901160426
43192CB00007B/1017